P9-DXO-660

WHAT
SHE
WROTE

Happy birthday Madge!

Dec 2020

WHAT
SHE
WROTE

AN ANTHOLOGY OF
WOMEN'S VOICES

Lilith House Press
Estes Park, Colorado

What She Wrote: An Anthology of Women's Voices

Copyright © 2020 Lilith House Press

Introduction copyright © 2020 Anna Blake, Crissi McDonald

All rights reserved. No part of this book may be reproduced or transmitted in any form or by any means, electronic or mechanical, including photocopying and recording, or by any information storage and retrieval systems, without the proper written permission of the copyright owner unless such copying is expressly permitted by federal copyright law. Lilith House Press is not authorized to grant permission for further uses of copyrighted selections printed or reprinted in this book without permission of their owners. Permission must be granted by individual copyright owners as identified herein. Reviewers may quote brief passages in a review. For permission requests or for more information, please contact Lilith House Press at https://www.lilithhousepress.com/contact.html.

ISBN 978-1-7353387-0-5 (print)
ISBN 978-1-7353387-1-2 (ebook)

Library of Congress Control Number 2020914082

Printed in the United States of America

Cover art: Carissa Sorensen
Cover Design: Jane Dixon Smith/ jdsmith-design.com
Editor: Birch Bark Editing, MaxieJane Frazier, Cat Parnell www.birchbarkediting.com

"Red" by Eve Allen. Copyright @ 2020. • "Kintsukuroi" by Lori Araki. Copyright @ 2020. • "The Music of Connection" by Nicole Artz. Copyright @ 2020. • "Wyoming Suite" by Sarah Virginia Barnes. Copyright @ 2020. • "That Saturday," "My Words," "Dream Horse" by Lasell Jaretzki Bartlett. Copyright @ 2020. • "Funeral Interrupted," "A Long Time Since," "The Broom Bearer and the Witch" by patti brehler. Copyright @ 2020. • "Twelfth Night (Notes from January 6)," "The Rulebreaker," "Excuses in Deer Season" by Kate Bremer. Copyright @ 2020. • "Poverty of Hope" by Wendi A. Clouse. Copyright @ 2020. • "Lizzy," "The Flies," "Alarm Clock" by Joanna Savage Coleman. Copyright @ 2020. • "Donkey Down," "La Notte," "The Seed" by Linda Doughty. Copyright @ 2020. • "Riding Through," "The Voices Within" by Elaine Kirsch Edsall. Copyright @ 2020. • "Sweet Muzzle," "Field of Foals," "Undomesticated" by Cynthia Funk. Copyright @ 2020. • "Up to My Knees in Water," "Aunt Bobbie's Place" by Kimberly Griffin. Copyright @ 2020. • "An English Woman's View of America," "A Story from England," "Nan and Granddad How" by Sue Hill. Copyright @ 2020. • "Shame Quarantine" by Susan Hannah Hull. Copyright @ 2020. • "Callings" by Marian Kelly. Copyright @ 2020. • "First Fire" by Elizabeth Love Kennon. Copyright @ 2020. • "Promenade," "Among the Horses" by Chris Kent. Copyright @ 2020. • "The Rooster Sanctuary" by Susan Ketchen. Copyright @ 2020. • "Journey of a Sacred Passage Doula," "Connection" by Amanda Jane Laramore. Copyright @ 2020. • "That Huge Engine," "Thievery" by Abby Letteri. Copyright @ 2020. • "Milk and Sugar," "Sorry About That!" by Ann Levy. Copyright @ 2020. • "Dear Women" by Kristina Margaret. Copyright @ 2020. • "A Fall in Three States," "Heritage," "What Happens After It Happens" by Crissi McDonald. Copyright @ 2020. • "Daughter to Mother," "Women in Literary Desire," "Smelling the Best" by Mary McGinnis. Copyright @ 2020. • "The Road to Buck," "4 A.M." by Kate McLaughlin. Copyright @ 2020. • "Truth Serum Horse," "Young Pup," "Animals are Lucky" by Tessa Pagones. Copyright @ 2020. • "Groovy" by Celeste Reich. Copyright @ 2020. • "Are You in There?" "May 15th," "October 22nd" by Alyssa Revels. Copyright @ 2020. • "The End of the Story" by Paula Romanow. Copyright @ 2020. • "How to Be," "To the Men Who Tried to Love Me," "Deathwatch" by Louise Thayer. Copyright @ 2020. • "And So It Began," "Awaken," "Busy" by Lauren Woodbridge. Copyright @ 2020. • "The Note I Found in a Jar," "Tap Tap Tap," "The Swing" by Kirsten Elizabeth Yeager. Copyright @ 2020.

Lilith House Press

Editorial Note: The styles used in this collection are consistent with each author's country of origin.

CONTENTS

INTRODUCTION

What She Wrote: An Anthology of Women's Voices is the creation of women who have written what is in their hearts and minds. You will find not only seasoned authors in this anthology but also women who've kept their words enclosed in a journal. Women who've set their words free in a blog. Women who have dreamed of seeing their words in print, and women who are secret poetry writers.

We believe that all writing takes courage to share. Writing has the potential to be revolutionary and can connect us to other human beings in ways other mediums cannot. We believe each and every woman who has offered a part of themselves to this anthology has a right to be here, and her voice has a right to be heard.

Read about what is important to them, whether it is family, horses, nature or their unique life adventures. They share their joys as well as their private grief. Through each author, you'll visit different parts of the USA as well as Australia, Canada, England, New Zealand, Scotland, South Africa, and Wales.

We are publishing this during Covid19, the George Floyd demonstrations, and a time when our very earth feels as though it is wobbling on its axis. Old ideas are being re-examined and thrown out to make room for the new. New ways of seeing also take courage, and within these pages we hope to offer you the world fresh from the eyes of each woman.

Anna Blake
Crissi McDonald
Lilith House Press

VOICES RAISED

*It only takes one voice, at the right pitch,
to start an avalanche.*

Dianna Hardy

THE BROOM BEARER AND THE WITCH

PATTI BREHLER

It's not often I find myself on a mountain with a witch.

Dressed in flowing black robes, she was tall and lean with skin painted green, and her gnarled hands clutched a brown paper bag and a wicker broom. A wide-brimmed hat, perched on her shock of white hair, barely cleared the door of the train as she stooped out. Her well-worn hiking boots hit the ground at Mountain View Siding with a bounce. I bounced out after her.

Several yards up the trail we turned to watch the Pike's Peak Cog Rail Train jerk away and waved at the gaping tourists until it passed out of view.

"Will you hold my broom?" she asked, "I really need to pee." And stepped off the trail to hike up her skirts.

How did I end up in the Colorado wilderness, broom-bearer for a witch straight from the Wizard of Oz? I was the oldest (and only woman) student at the Barnett Bicycle Institute's Elite Technician course in Colorado Springs. My husband and I determined that certification would give our bike store's service department an edge. Why me and not him? He knew business, following a traditional career path. I knew bikes and followed my hands—learning a machinist trade supported my thirst for motion.

Barnett's course was six days of hands-on-learning, with a mid-week break on

Halloween. My young classmates looked forward to a Devil's Night on the town; I looked for an adventure. The Pike's Peak Cog Railway out of Manitou Springs was making its last run of the year on Halloween. I meant to be there, never expecting to land in partnership with a witch.

The train left at nine. Up before dawn, I grabbed my pack and hiked five up-hill miles

from my hotel in a biting drizzle. Fog poured from the mountainside, shrouding the treetops along Ruxton Creek. The red-roofed cog rail station nestled in the hills of Englemann Canyon at 6500 feet elevation. When I bought my ticket, a hand-drawn trail map on the counter almost leapt into my hands.

"I'll take this, too," I said to the clerk.

It wasn't the greatest map I ever saw, but it was a map. And it gave me a mad-as-a-hatter spark of an idea. Could I get off at the summit and hike down?

Diesel engines rumbled. The train lurched forward as the gear wheel underneath it

engaged with a rack between the rails. The energy necessary to drag two full passenger cars up a grade steeper than a conventional train could handle, shuddered through rigid laminate chairs bolted to the floor. With no pulling engine, the view through all-around windows was unrestricted.

I didn't expect much of a view with the dismal weather, but the witch chatting with the conductor at the front of the crowded car caught my attention. Was the altitude affecting me?

Was the rail gauge lined with yellow bricks?

I edged closer to eavesdrop.

"Well, now, Peggy," the conductor said, "with snow preventing us from reaching the

summit, we'll be reversing at Windy Point today." No summit? There go my plans to hike down.

"That will only give you about an hour and a half to get back to Mountain View."

"That'll be fine, John," the witch said. "I just need to get to Barr Camp to trick-or-treat

Chuck and Cathy's two little ones. I won't be staying long, and I'll hustle right back."

Wait—she's getting off the train? I studied my simple map. Yep, there was Barr Camp, right on the trail from Pike's Peak summit.

I inched to the seat behind Witch Peggy, who entertained a young family. She was gentle

with a toddler snuggled up to her mother's leg, not sure what to think of this green-faced hag. I leaned forward. "Excuse me. I was wondering…"

Her green beak turned to consider me. "Yes?"

"I couldn't help but overhear you talking to the conductor, and…"

"I'm going to trick-or-treat the winter caretakers' children at Barr Camp."

"Yes. Are you familiar with the trail down the mountain?"

Her eyes sparkled. "You could say so."

"Well, I have this map and hoped to hike it."

"You got good shoes?" She leaned around the seat to catch sight of my feet. I stuck my

right muddy Merrell hiking boot into the aisle. She bent closer, her eyes casing me as if she were a genuine witch trying to determine if I was demon or faerie.

"And I have my backpack with extra clothes and water." I held out the map. "Is the trail

well-marked?"

"Yes, it's easy enough to follow. I'm getting off at Mountain View, from there it's a mile and a half hike to Barr Trail." She swung back and yelled, "John! This here gal wants to get off with me at the siding." John nodded.

The cog train crept through a forest of Englemann and Colorado blue spruce and

Ponderosa pines. A top speed of nine miles per hour allowed

for relaxed sightseeing, if there was anything at all to see through the low-lying clouds. John pointed out Minnehaha Falls. We had to take his word for it.

At 8000 feet, temperatures dropped and mist iced tree limbs and boulders lining the track.

At 9500 feet, we broke through the clouds and there it was— Pike's Peak. A magnificent, snow-covered glare against the deep blue sky of high altitude. Sunshine blinded us, we responded with a collective "ahh."

Witch Peggy learned why I came to Colorado from Michigan and that I had experience

wilderness hiking. (I once started an "adventure coaching" business with a promising start; I ended up marrying my trial client after a five-day hike on the Appalachian Trail.) I learned Peggy was 73 and lived many years here, roaming these mountains. We learned we each got married at age 38, the call of adventure keeping us unattached until then. Like old friends reacquainting, we both got an inkling of destiny.

"I arranged this Halloween trip weeks ago," she said. "My friend was going to join me and we'd hike down. But this morning she called and said she was too sick."

"I'm sorry."

"Don't be sorry. Yes, I was disappointed. With the weather and all, I wasn't comfortable going it alone. Say, I have an idea." She winked. "If you're up for it."

I'm always up for ideas.

"If you come with me to Barr Camp, I'll hike down the trail with you. That way I can do

what I planned, with you as my companion, and then I'll show you the way."

The rabbit hole opened.

So there I was, like a witch's familiar, carrying her broom in the wilderness lap of Pike's

Peak on our way to trick-or-treat. On the narrow trail to camp we gained 200 feet of elevation. Not much conversation passed between us, in keeping with the hiker's creed to respect each other's private commune with nature.

The youngsters squealed when they spotted Witch Peggy with her wrinkled brown bag trudging to their native-log cabin. "Trick-or-treat!" And off they ran with their loot. Peggy chatted with Chuck and Cathy long enough to make sure supplies were getting delivered on time.

Winter is long in the mountains. We were below the tree line, but still had seven miles to

descend back to Manitou Springs. Time to go. At a hand-hewn wooden bridge over a snaking, dribbling creek, we waved goodbye to the winter family.

"That was fun," I twirled with arms uplifted. "And what a beautiful day here above the clouds."

We could see for miles, a shocking contrast to the miserable weather beneath the clouds.

It was below freezing, but sunshine and fellowship warmed my soul. Here the trail was wide enough to walk abreast; Witch Peggy pointed out features in the distance. "There's Mount Manitou far ahead to the left, and Eagle Mountain to the right. And closer, beyond the cog track, is Pilot's Knob. But, oh my, I shouldn't be talking so much. It's a hiker's right to silence."

"No, don't stop. This is great." My words unleashed a deluge.

For this witch was Peggy Par, mountaineer extraordinaire, one-time field leader with the

El Paso County Search and Rescue. In 1981, on Cutler Mountain while watching red-tailed hawks, Peggy spotted a woman fall from a cliff. She ran for help and the responding rescue team brought her along to identify the location. The woman survived. Assisting the rescue bewitched Peggy; even at age 59 she was more than ready to jump when the leader asked her to join the team.

She told me of risky rescues. In a quiet voice she spoke of sometimes finding only bodies. Her adrenaline at the first call for help, the team camaraderie, her exhaustion after nights and days of searching, spilled onto me. Like me, challenges and non-traditional roles filled her life.

At Lightning Point, an aerie ledge a quick scramble off the trail, Witch Peggy shared her

wheat-bread peanut butter sandwich and I shared my water. We split her homemade chocolate chip cookie. Pike's Peak loomed behind us; below, clouds hid city bustle. We pointed and smiled, chatted and sighed, just me and Peggy, broom-bearer and witch, witnessing mountain rapture.

Off again, we strolled on a rare, level, and straight section of trail. Witch Peggy giggled.

"Last summer I was hiking along here, and I looked up to see a backpacker coming toward me. He didn't notice me right away, and I stopped. Because there he was, naked as a jaybird from the waist down. Except, of course, his socks and boots."

"What did you do?"

"I started whistling. That got his attention. He hustled off the trail, dropped his pack, and pulled his pants back on."

I couldn't walk for my hysterics, imagining the embarrassment the young man felt when Peggy strode by him with a knowing smile and wave hello.

We descended into clouds and entered an ice-laden Hansel and Gretel forest, wind chiming the sparkling branches. Our gaiety quieted as we planted our feet on icy rocks. I kept close, still carrying the witch's broom. A quick grab prevented Peggy from a fall when she mis- stepped.

"So, who is here for who?" She patted my hand. Soon she was clenching my arm for support along steep switchbacks approaching No Name Creek. Perhaps, on the train, Witch Peggy thought I needed a guide. Perhaps, after our communion on the mountain, she saw me as her familiar—a witch's spirit-in-aide.

I felt honored.

Temperatures rose as altitude dropped. The dense forest still dripped, but the trail was no longer icy. Good thing. Thirteen treacherous switchbacks stood between us and the end of Barr Trail. We managed them together, without incident, grateful for the wood fence that kept us funneled on the path. After nearly five hours, our hike drew to a close.

"Where is your hotel?" Witch Peggy asked as we stepped back to reality and I handed back her broom.

"Five miles from here, off Ore Mill Drive."

"Well, that's on my way home. I'll drive you."

I was glad to rest my feet and delay this magical encounter. Our damp bodies fogged the interior of her car as we drove away in twilight.

THE VOICES WITHIN

ELAINE KIRSCH EDSALL

Cathy the Counsellor must have a magnetic memory where everything sticks, because the only thing I've ever seen her write down is the next appointment date. She also has the brownest eyes and wears coral lipstick that suits her complexion perfectly.

The counselling room and its furnishings have changed little during the years we've been talking. Cathy's had a few different hairstyles in our time together, and I've had a few different cancers; active, remissive, progressive and more recently, incurable. We talk about them all, shake them up and calm them down. We talk diversely about grief, relationships, anger, baking, sex and horses. Spread things out, sketch them, laugh at them, rant and swear at them. No emotions remain unexplored.

In my first counselling sessions I saw Christine; it was my fourth cancer recurrence, and I was having combined chemotherapy/platinum therapy treatment. The accompanying high-dose steroids initiated a mental meltdown. I'd never seen a counsellor before, I thought counselling was for weak people. Christine helped me understand why I had unravelled, and because I was incapable of clear thought (I couldn't even stop sobbing) I followed her suggestions by rote. We began with simple breathing exercises, and a year later I was comfortable enough in my own skin to discard my suit of armour, and ceremonially dump it in the waste-paper basket. That year gave me the insight for Post Traumatic Growth.

That year probably saved my life.

I have a friend who is a narcissistic drama queen. She's also incredibly kind. I make the rookie error of trusting her, before I discover the basis of our friendship is my usefulness -and as that diminishes the friendship wanes. She also has penchant for distorting the truth; when I question her about a certain event, it doesn't go well. The more defensive she gets, the more frustrated I feel until, with a single intake of breath, I explode in a torrent that surprises even me. I don't know who is most shocked. I'd spoken with blatant honesty, but people don't want home truths. Your truth isn't theirs. I beat myself up about it big time because it had happened before; similar harshness, just different scenarios.

So, I ask Cathy "Why do I sabotage reasonable friendships, knowing the consequences will be detrimental. And afterwards feel incredibly free but horribly remorseful?"

Talking for an hour shows there's no neat answer. Cathy asks me if I've heard about sub-personality/voice dialogue counselling. She outlines the principle and suggests I consider it.

I Google the basics of Voice Dialogue Counselling at home but quit when the explanation gets too wordy. Despite always aiming to be the star pupil, I arrive at our next session without pre-thought answers. Cathy explains in simple detail how the therapy works and reiterates that I can stop anytime. With a deep breath (and trepidation), I settle into familiar relaxed poise and we begin.

"Hello" she says, with smiling eyes. "Who's brought you here, who is sitting here today?"

"Elaine" I reply, shifting my feet and hands. "Elaine, the grown-up. Elaine takes care of everything. Sorts everyone out, gets them there on time." The words flow easily, without fore-thought.

"Elaine the parent?"

"No, not a parent, an adult".

"What else does Elaine do?"

"Weeeeeell . . . she presents a persona to the world; shows how she wants to be seen by everyone else…and by herself. She talks to people, receives information, keeps her composure. Stays positive, gets meals on the table. She runs everything day-to-day, she's very organised."

"Does she ever get tired? Drop her guard?"

"She tries not to. People rely on her positive appearance." I stop and think for a moment before adding, "I rely on it too."

"How does is make Elaine feel, people relying on her?"

"Sometimes she feels really pressured. She can't just dump the dishes in the sink and read a book. She wants everything perfect, not affected by cancer, not let cancer stop her doing what she wants, and she thinks other people expect that too."

"And do they?"

I shrug because I don't want to admit they don't. It's only me who expects it, only me.

"Probably not," I concede with a mumble.

Cathy nods. "Would you mind if we let Elaine have a rest now? We can speak again later."

As Cathy suggests I take some deep breaths, I stretch my arms, and realise how tightly I'm holding myself. I laugh, and wriggle, and say how strange it feels, talking about myself as if I was another person, a person with an independent voice but my thoughts. The other Elaine feels much more confident than me, certainly more in control. I'd really like to get to know her better. Cathy asks if I'd like to continue, and if someone else would like a voice?

"Yeah," I answer, slumping back in the chair. I feel a defiant scowl spread across my face. "I'm important. I'll tell it straight."

"Who are you?" Cathy asks politely

"PRICKLY!!" The name practically spits itself out. (Is this really me?) I'm glaring at Cathy, daring her to flinch.

"What do you do, Prickly?"

"I set the record straight. Do the dirty work. I see through them; someone has to tell them what they've done. They patronise her and feel sorry for her and she hates that. Or else they ignore her completely with that ooooh-I-didn't-know-what-to-say crap. She says she's used to it by now, but I know she isn't. The people who say 'oh, I thought you were a survivor' or 'you used to be so strong' I remember it. I tell them how much it hurt. They don't get another chance."

"That's a big job, Prickly." Cathy continues, as if polite conversation with this angst-ridden teenager part of me was an everyday occurrence.

As Prickly's personality spews out, not exactly speaking tongues and vomiting green bile but clearly the voice of my harsh mouth, I feel quite shocked. I never knew Prickly existed. My shock shows because Cathy raises an eyebrow and a hand and asks if I'd like a break. I nod reply.

"OK Prickly," she says, "thank you for having your say. We're taking a break now and can come back to you later."

My eyes feel like they're out on stalks, my jaw has dropped down to my knees. I look blankly at Cathy and exhale the biggest breath.

"Prickly the Fastest Tongue in the West" I say slowly, and a giggle rises up, popping out like an unexpected fart, and while the laughter lightens Prickly's impact, Cathy and I mull over his characteristics until I'm ready to continue.

"Who would like to speak next?" asks Cathy gently.

Sitting opposite each other in comfortable silence, we wait, until a little voice says "Me please, me. Vulnerable."

I'm as startled by Vulnerable's meekness as I was by Prickly's bravado and notice my shoulders have rounded into a protective shell, and I'm lowering both my face and my gaze.

"Hello Vulnerable," says Cathy, once again talking as naturally as if she was speaking to a friend. "Is it ok to call you Vulnerable, or is there another name you prefer?"

"Vulnerable is fine. It's what they call me...when they bother to acknowledge me."

"Who are 'they', Vulnerable?"

"The big ones. The other ones who talk all the time. I never get to speak. Sometimes I try, I want to tell them I'm frightened and scared of what might happen, but they laugh, and say I must be jolly and positive, and Elaine gets cross and tuts, and Prickly threatens to kick me. So I don't say it anymore. But it's horrible when I feel sad."

"Does anyone listen to you, Vulnerable?"

"No not really."

"Do you have anyone you can talk to?"

"No not really, except maybe Steel Core. She doesn't ever say much but she's always there, always there for everyone."

"Where is she now?"

"Right next to me. Next to my shoulder."

"So, you're leaning on her?"

"Yes, we all lean on her. She's wide so we all fit. And she makes a shadow if you need it so you can shelter underneath, but it's only me that does that"

"Do you think we could we speak to Steel Core when you've finished? Is there anything else you'd like to tell us?"

"I've said enough things. More than they've let me say before." Vulnerable sounds quite drained. There's a pause, before she adds "Will they remember I'm here?"

"We'll remind them, Vulnerable" replies Cathy "We'll all hear you now because you're Important. You're just as important as the others."

Vulnerable lifts her gaze, looks Cathy in the eyes and straightens her shoulders. "Thank you, Cathy," she says quietly. "Thank you for making me Important."

Wow. Wow and probably another wow. Who knew? I'm sitting straight and tall as Steel Core comes to the fore.

"Hello Steel Core" says Cathy with continued ease. "Vulnerable suggested you speak; she says you protect her."

"I protect them all," replies a steady, unemotional voice. "That's why I'm here, at the core. I am Core of Steel."

"And is that the name you prefer?"

"Yes please."

"Are you just a shelter for the others, Core of Steel?"

"No. I run the length of her body; I am the backbone, solid and invincible. Chemotherapy doesn't corrode me, drugs can't tarnish me, and I don't double-up in pain or slump in defeat. I'm a pole for the others to dance around, to lean on . . . and there's always a lot of leaning."

"How long have you been there?"

"I've been here forever. As a child, Elaine was her mum's confidante, her ally in a troubled marriage. Elaine started to bend under the weight and have panic attacks, so I came to help then. I've held her up ever since."

"Do you ever get tired?"

"No, I sleep upright. I'm on call 24/7."

"Is your voice heard?"

"I don't need a voice, I don't have opinions, I am just here. Being here is enough for me. They move closer when they need me, I don't go find them."

"Are there a lot of personalities around you, Core of Steel?"

"Yes. A few are permanent, some of them come and go, and some of them job-share because they're not always needed."

"Who job-shares?" asks Cathy, and I could swear a hint of a smile crosses her lips. I'm sitting listening like I'm tuned into reality TV, like this is all playing out in front of me, and I forget that I'm part of it.

"People-Pleaser and People-Saver job-share. They used to work close together, so they get on fine. Fence-Mender and Apologiser job-share too. They leaned a lot in the old days, but I don't see very much of them now."

"Are you happy as you are, are you happy with what you do, Core of Steel?"

"Yes...and yes. Sometimes I wonder what it would be like to wriggle, maybe bend a bit, but I'm so deeply rooted, so entrenched, it's not possible."

"How does that make you feel?"

"I try to lean on myself a bit, and if that doesn't work, instead of moaning about what I can't do, I try and change how I think about it. I have a lot of time to think"

"Is changing the perspective difficult for you?"

"It was at the start because I only face one way, but I've had a lot of practice now. Having stable roots and people who need you and knowing where you fit . . . it's not such a bad life."

"Thanks for telling us all this, Core of Steel. Is there any more you want to say?"

"No, I'm pretty much done, but I'm always here if you come back"

Cathy looks at the clock, I take some tissues and wipe my eyes. Then, reaching my hand behind my back I trace a finger down my backbone and silently thank Core of Steel. We've lived so closely all these years, but never met. Now it all starts to make sense.

"A week . . . two weeks?" asks Cathy, picking up her diary.

"Two weeks please, I need time to process all this!"

"So, you'd like to do some more." It's a statement more than a question and requires no answer.

We chitchat, schedule the next date, hug, and I leave the room. The voices come with me. They are me.

There're more voices to hear, personalities to discover, interactions to observe. After just this first session I feel more complete, more me, and being me feels enough. I even feel a touch of admiration. As Core of Steel says, "there's something to be said for knowing where you fit."

POVERTY OF HOPE

WENDI CLOUSE

Plain dominates my field of vision.

Not sun-kissed, prairie-dirt golden plain
lighting the morning,
but the nondescript handshake-from-the-plastic-brotherhood,
synthetic beige
slapped on everything for unification. Created for acceptance
in lieu of scrutiny,
a lurid hair shirt of pallor.

Contaminating everything

in its noise with a signaled sly endorsement
of plain approval.
Then darkness arrives,
without pomp or proclamation, sliding through cracks from a
second-rate city.
Home to Hondas and hamburgers and
masses cheering in ignorance

don't tread on me

while sweet smoke undetected
settles. Smothering anger burning cold in the back of my throat.
Overcome, with no way—forward,
rage picked up at Walmart
with groceries,
and dirty socks, and dirty dishes, and the

poverty of dirty hope.

Just another day
pissed to nothingness
demanding retreat
-capitulate-
it-just-doesn't matter memories
tempered with things-never-change-deliberation.

I have what I deserve.

My earned value appraised and tendered
through endemic eyes
hissing
beauty-as-currency exchanged for survival.
Bright-razor brilliance
is a pejorative swung aptly with the intent

to maim

from a once-blonde, white-bread girl, sideways looking back-biter
stealing words of dreams
right out of my mouth
while I eat with guilt, alone.
She laughs because I'd rather read a book
than entertain them with the target of

my insides.

So—quiet words—crumble.
I am erased to silence
with the blur of
too hot vodka
swallowed between the
second shift and sticky longing again.

Darkness appears,

today without pomp,
between dog food and detergent
with blistering feet in my lousy shoes in the front seat of a
Honda,
praising every awkward contradiction,
demanding I stop
any scramble forward toward

change.

ALARM CLOCK

JOANNA SAVAGE COLEMAN

I wake up and it's all a dream.

I wish I could go back to sleep.

Back there under the gold-rinsed horizon. Together. Drips of red watercolour fade into pink and lick the crests of the tide as it ripples out to sea. The six of us. The last six humans there ever were. The sand shifts and squeaks under our bare feet. The grains gather and compact around our heels, holding us then letting us go. The beach stretches to the edge of where my vision blurs; a damp bandage rolled out behind me. Like washed linen cleaned of its previous crusts and wounds.

I love these people more than I have the cognition to recognise. It threatens to expand and burst through the soft mucous that wraps my brain every time I dare to think about it. My physical form is inadequate to hold these emotions. I'm an endless, cavernous, blown-glass vase containing the sum of the universe. I harbor, within my skin, the scattered souls of everyone who ever was. They dance around the ever-growing wilderness and wasteland, forever finding their way back to us. Condensing into us. Just us six. Six inadequate blown-glass vases fashioned of blood and bone, containing the sum of everyone who ever was. We are gods in this place. The birds clatter about in the trees. The dew is settling where the undergrowth begins.

There's a boat on the beach. A half-submerged shipwreck.

I feel the excitement of every adventurer who ever lived. I'm charged with electric pulsing energy, drawing in from the air around me and lifting me up where I walk weightlessly onto the deck. I feel the others float around me. She puts a hand on my shoulder as we travel down the stairway into the bowels of the ship. The air becomes cool and wet. I feel the love of everyone who ever felt love spill from her palm into my shoulder. We are connected like two locations on a map by a train-line. I think my heart will rise to the point it stops beating. But it doesn't. I'm weeping. A smile that belongs to millions meets the eyes of millions at once. Ecstasy. We travel deeper inside the boat. Its timber ribs jut out at angles, worn smooth by the water, then roughened by the blanket of barnacles and shelled creatures who barely shrink from us as we pass by.

We had to come here. The only things we can experience now are things no one who ever was has known before. Things unseen. We search the ship, picking apart every tiny corner. Every splinter of wood. Digging in towards the centre of it. We are searching for the one thing no one who ever was has experienced. A reason to keep on. The hull groans softly to the tide as it nudges the decomposing wood, the flaking pale-blue paint. We step down. The water surges around my ankles, cool and thick with salt. I feel the recognition of everyone who ever stood in cold water. Feel it push and pull. Feel it tug at me to follow then let me go. I feel the excitement of everyone who never stood like this. The trepidation. I feel the fear. The anger. The loss. Bad things happened here. To some people. The tide tugs at them to follow it out, but they won't go. It's safe here, and we all want to find the same thing. Drowning is not a new experience. Not for some.

I wake defensive. My muscles tensed before I have the opportunity to control them. The alarm isn't going off yet, but I know it will and that knowledge fills me with despair for a moment. The despair of a child I think briefly, then it's gone. I don't want to go to work. I pick up my phone and squint at the screen. Seven minutes before the alarm. I lay back. That's not enough time to fall sleep again. The boat rocks from side to side as though buffeted by a whisper. I hear the others behind me. Shifting about. Searching. Weeeee-o-weeeee-o the alarm screeches at me. I'm shocked from sleep. This time my body is soft and limp. I feel so exhausted, but I let the alarm play as I drag myself up through the sheets. My feet touch the hard ground. They feel swollen and dry. I feel picked apart, reduced down to just the simple facets of myself. Nothing more than what I've experienced. A husk stretched thin. Back in the real world with everyone scattered into millions of pieces, I feel so alone.

The pipes groan and the shower splutters awake. First, it's too cold, then too hot. My mind is bored. I've experienced all this before. I don't eat breakfast. I've eaten it all before and it tires me. I travel the same journey to work. Same pass key. Same locker. Same mug. One sugar, then milk. They ask me how I am, and I reply the same way I always do: "I'm good thanks. How are you?" I don't catch their reply. The photo copier is jammed, and I don't have time to reset it. Up to the other office to use theirs. I'm stopped in the hallway. Someone asks me something and the answer comes before I can acknowledge it. They smile and thank me. I must have got it right.

I think of the boat while I'm washing my hands. The cold water. Did I find what I was looking for? I need to go back. But I don't know how to dream like that. I only have a dream like that once in a decade. And I haven't been alive long enough to know it's a pattern for sure. The interim spent repeating and forgetting and replacing the spaces in my memories with less important material. Will I keep on for ten years to fall back into the shipwreck? A decade before I feel the tin cups jostle away from my touch as I search behind them for something never seen nor experienced by any human who ever was? I don't know. I begin the process of forgetting. I set my alarm again. This time, I hope to stay asleep.

UP TO MY KNEES IN WATER

KIMBERLY GRIFFIN

Knee-deep water Oh my

My sleep saturated instincts tell me something is very wrong. I think I hear a sound that is wrong. Lapping waves, check ... wind, check. It is an alarm. The insistent squawk of a bilge pump alarm. Oh, argh.

We up-anchored yesterday to find a cove that would offer us protection from the winds and waves that would be generated by the force of the wind. We had considered three separate weather reports. We are anchored in a protected bay on the island of Pserimos in the Dodecanese Islands, Greece, in the Eastern Mediterranean Sea about seven miles west of the Turkish coast.

Winds are fluky here and storms subject to radical change. We have been sailing together for a decade, and we are easy with our knowledge of each other's strengths.

I slither in a backwards crab crawl out of our bunk and brace a foot against the opposite bulkhead to decelerate my three-foot drop to the sole (floor). The contours of the hull dictated that our double bunk be at chest height with only twenty inches of head room.

Therefore, the slither out.

I grab David's foot and quietly say, "David, David we have a bilge pump alarm, I am going to check the aft cabin." I scamper over the sole hatch covering the bilge and engine room in the main cabin, through the cockpit and throw open the aft cabin companion way hatch.

Oh bother—water up to my knees.

David has the sole hatch cleared in the main cabin to reveal way too much water in the bilge that is about to challenge our engine and electrical system.

All hands on deck—wait it is just us! And we are here. We have a few words and get to work. David uses every mechanical pump we have as well as one manual, and me: the low-tech, one-woman bucket bail.

Did I tell you it is 2am and the wind is howling about 40 knots on our nose with green water over the bow (cool sailor talk for waves breaking over the front of the boat)?

The anchor is holding.

We have cabin lights, but it is really dark on deck and in the cockpit and we are working frantically to clear the water. We have three hulls, the two outer ones reinforced with foam, as she is a trimaran and will not likely sink, but, without the engine we cannot move her away from the rocks on shore the wind has lined us up to land on.

We are close to each other, on either side of the aft cabin companion way, David using a manual pump in the aft cabin and accessing the cockpit drains to clear the water he is pumping. The full buckets he hands to me I empty overboard. We have eye conversations to reassure each other.

We are about two hours into this adventure.

Faint morning light is erasing the stars and we can clearly see how close to shore we are. We stop bailing for a wee rest and discuss our options.

The shore is close if all else fails we can likely get to land. We cannot abandon our boat … Can we? We are near exhaustion and cannot get to the thru hull that failed and is letting the wave action back wash into the hull as fast as we remove it. We both let out a collective expletive or two. Have another eye conversation. David pumps and bails and I put together the ditch bag.

Passports, boat documents, dry warm clothing, water sandals, money and some valuables, water, a bit of food and matches into a small dry bag. We could don life vests and likely make it ashore.

We have been sailing together for more than ten years on three different boats, on many seas, oceans and geography. We found this one-off, well designed and over-built-girl-in-need-of-attention trimaran in Tunisia, North Africa and limped her back to Malta for a two-year refit.

Paring her down to her bones, we rebuilt her to suit just the two of us. We adopted the cute phrase, she drinks six, feeds four and sleeps two. We prefer short handing, which means just the two of us relying on each other, no crew.

David designed the interior to fit us, literally, he drafted to scale and was constantly measuring me, hip to knee and shoulder to elbow to get the settee correct and counter tops in the galley correct.

We hired a shipwright in Holland to build a mockup of the interior that we traveled to Holland to spend time in and to stand in and, making needed changes.

At one point I was discussing a wee bit of stairway, to a pantry and asked if the top stair could be a seat for me to use when cooking. He politely asked if he could measure my bum, and he did.

The finished pieces were shipped in containers to Malta and installed by the shipwright, and his crew over the course of 18 months.

I adopted and fed them all. As you do.

She is seaworthy, comfortable, and reliably welcoming to guests. Well she does sport cheetah print cockpit cushions for pity sake. As you have to board her from the aft swim step and scamper under the boom over the aft deck to access the ample cockpit, you must also tread on the cushions—the first cream colored cushions were ruined in a season.

We found this amazing woven cheetah print that works

really well to hide footprints and also plays nicely with teak wood, cork decking, cream paint, white sails, deep-yellow boot stripe, and yellow canvas sail covers. It is just such a surprise for our cocktail guests. They are never sure if it is fun or really bad taste. We love to watch their expressions as they board this atypical boat and meet us.

So, we are having a breather: the water is still coming in, the pumps are making a bit of difference, but not much. David looks me in the eye and says, "Sit tight," and disappears down a hatch.

Okay, I wait.

He emerges with a big grin and says, "I think this is the time to give you these," with a flat jewelry box in his wet hand. I am incredulous and also smiling and shaking my head at his ridiculous timing.

You see we have had a running joke. As boats require ongoing maintenance and considerable parts, we are barraged, while in port, with ordered parts coming in boxes and parcels.

As all boats are referred to as her, and she, I mocked jealousy and occasionally accepted the delivery of parcels with the phrase "I suppose these are my pearls?"

And that was what was in the box. Oh My. I am overwhelmed so I do what I always do: cry and snot and blabber and kiss my dear man.

Then we continue to bail.

We have a confab and decide that we might be able to weigh the anchor and power out of the bay, if our engine and electrical is above water. So we clear more water and start the engine. She runs. Exhale. Sigh. And we man our well-worn stations.

David is on the bow to engage the windlass, the power grinder that pulls in the anchor chain.

Water is breaking over the bow and the wind is full on our nose, David is bracing. I am at the helm, watching my David and keeping us pointed into the wind. If we catch wind on a side, we will be compromised and lose our way on or forward momentum.

We need to ease forward to take tension off the anchor chain so the windlass can roll the chain and deposit it in the forepeak.

It is a cat and mouse game keeping us steady and into the wind without putting undue stress on the windlass, less she fails, or over burdens the engine.

From my helm position I can read the wind direction by the way it hits my face and breaks on either side of my nose. I cannot see the angle of the anchor chain below the bow and into the water, so David gives hand signals to let me know the direction we need to keep tracking and how much slack the windlass needs. I am also aware of my man on the bow of our boat that is being battered by waves and the motion they create.

The anchor is up, and David gives the hand signal that we are clear. I move the throttle forward to gain way and beat the wind punching us back, but not too much throttle as we need this engine.

Our anchorage was on the far side of a fish farm. Oh bother. The fish farms have netting held up by metal buoys and there is a zig zag path thru these hull-crunching buoys.

Argh.

I grip the wheel and steam a considered course. David makes his way from the fore deck into the cockpit and ducks down to the engine room and the pumps and the pressure gages and all manner of necessary apparatus.

My job is to make it to the rocky point and turn to the right or starboard or south. So, I use the throttle and wheel to keep us nose into the wind.

I scream a little. No one can hear me with the engine and howling wind. Did I mention it is howling, and the water crashing over the bow? My concentration is steady. I must not get us side on to the wind. We will become a piece of wreckage without forward momentum. And slowly almost imperceptibly we are making way. I must use much more throttle than is prudent and I do.

We gradually pass through the fish farm and the point comes a little closer every moment.

As we pass that rocky point, I can see a white-washed Greek church standing proud and

surrounded by a split rail fence painted bright blue. I had had my eyes on that wee fine church and offered a bit of conversation to the Greek gods, some nice, some not so much. We pass the church and, as we turn, and are now downwind, all is suddenly quiet, the water is settled and there is a peace.

The water below decks is self-bailing because of the forward movement. David can leave the engine room and relives me of the helm. We kiss and laugh, and I go down to the galley to make steel-cut oat porridge with butter and sugar and pour us a dram each of rum. I wore pearls.

A STORY FROM ENGLAND (ALISON, EDNA, AND PETER)

SUE HILL

Alison

Alison was in her early 50's. Her husband had a well-paid job which afforded her the luxuries of not having to go out to work and a smart house in a nice neighbourhood. There was a sweeping, gravelled horseshoe drive in the front of the house and a large double garage in which two expensive cars snoozed. She always frowned when thinking about the driveway as it was usually cluttered with her son's scruffy Nissan Micra. The little car was old and grey and had more than a few dents and scrapes along its sides. The outlook from her kitchen window was completely spoilt by this hideous vehicle and she knew she was judged by the neighbours for having a less than pristine frontage. It was the sort of neighbourhood where curtains twitched, and whispers travelled far.

Alison's son was Peter. He was in his early 20's and was still living at home with his parents. He truly was a thorn in her side. He still acted like a teenager – he ate in his bedroom and never brought the dirty crockery downstairs. His hair was long and unkempt. Alison knew from the dirty washing that he wasn't changing his underwear every day and his room smelled musty and unclean. He would stomp upstairs in his dirty shoes, leaving mud on the clean, cream carpet. He hadn't ever had a steady job and was constantly asking for money. Goodness knows what he did with it all – she suspected he might be into "whacky baccy" or whatever they call it these days. At least he didn't smoke cigarettes. Well, not to her knowledge anyway. She dreamed of the day he would leave home, but she couldn't really imagine that it would ever be a possibility.

The other worry in her life, apart from household mess, her son and the awful car in the driveway was her mother, Edna. Ten years ago, when Alison's dad died, she'd agreed with her Mum that the family home was now much too big for her to cope with alone and they'd moved her into sheltered accommodation. She had a lovely little ground-floor flat with emergency pull cords in every room. Alison had great fun with her Mum, planning the decoration of the flat and installing a new kitchen and a new bathroom for her. Her Mum had actually been quite bossy at the time and was very insistent on choosing the decorations and furniture herself. Alison was feeling a little down– her husband had just gone back overseas, and Peter was being particularly difficult, so she didn't put up a fight with Edna.

Alison was concerned about her Mum. She was getting very forgetful. She'd managed to leave the kettle on the stove to boil dry, which could have caused a fire. She kept forgetting or saying the wrong words, and Alison was getting concerned that she would not be able to manage independent living for much longer. It was something she worried about daily. At night, when applying her expensive face creams before bed, she'd look at herself in the mirror and frown at the creases on her forehead, forgetting that the frowns were the cause of the creases. Another sigh and off to bed alone.

Peter

Peter was frustrated that he was stuck in the family home with no immediate prospect of escaping his Mum and setting up his own home. He spent every day in his room, on his computer, searching job sites for work. He'd have the occasional interview, but his lack of experience was the usual reason they gave for not employing him. He'd even tried the local burger bars—surely, he could get a job there—but no luck. The constant rejection was starting to get a bit depressing. But he'd give himself a pep-talk: "Come on, lad, keep on looking. There must be something out there." His Nan always made him feel better, consoling him with the fact that there are hundreds of people searching for each vacancy and it was the state of the economy rather than any personal failing that was stopping Peter from finding a job.

His Mum was also a cause of frustration. She was always getting on at him. He couldn't do anything right. If he went into the kitchen, she'd tut as if he were in the way. She was always too busy with housework to have a proper conversation—for goodness' sake—how many times does a countertop need to be cleaned in a day? It got to the point where he'd just eat in his room to avoid her constant nagging about his lack of a job, the length of his hair, the state of his car and his various other failings. If he went straight from the front door, up the stairs quickly to his room, he could manage to avoid her altogether. He'd wait until she was out of the house before taking all the dirty crocks down to the kitchen—although she'd usually moan at him about that by finding his stash before he was able to get them downstairs.

Peter loved his car. He'd bought it five years ago with money his Dad gave him on his 18th birthday. The car represented the immense feeling of freedom he'd felt: no more having to ask for lifts or explaining where he wanted to go. He actually felt a rather silly, sentimental attachment to it. His Nan offered to buy him a newer car but he thought he'd keep the old car running as long as he could as it was so cheap to run and he felt very uncomfortable at the thought of spending his Nan's money. His Mother kept him on a paltry allowance. She moaned every time she handed money over. "It's not like I spend it on weed or cigarettes or booze," he thought.

He always liked to take something to his Nan when he visited on a Tuesday and things were getting to be rather expensive. He had to pay for insurance and fuel for his car—he actually drove quite a few miles in his pursuit of employment opportunities. He wanted to get a haircut, but that was getting too expensive as well. He decided to wait until he'd either got a whiff of a new girlfriend opportunity, or an interview, before getting his hair cut again. It had been a while since he'd had either, sadly. His Mum was also too house-proud. He felt as though he couldn't breathe at home.

He really got an earful last time his parents had gone away. He had piled the dirty dishes next to the sink and planned to put them all in the dishwasher on the day they were due home. It seemed a waste of energy to use it during their absence – better to do it all in one go. He then got a phone call offering him a job interview the same day. He was in a panic showering and changing into some slightly smarter clothes. He'd wasted his time, of course as no job offer followed. And then, when he got home, he had to endure his mother screaming at him because it looked as though he hadn't done any housework since she'd been gone. He couldn't win.

His Nan knew the truth. She took the time to ask him questions and listen to the answers. She sat at the table with him at teatime and they had a conversation with eye contact and everything. No TV in the background. Nan would make helpful suggestions about job adverts she'd seen; point out where petrol was on special offer; and tell him if she'd spotted any "lovely young ladies" that might be in need of a Petey companion. The only thing Peter didn't like was when she offered him money—he felt really uncomfortable taking money from an elderly lady and did his best to resist.

Edna

Edna lived in a warden-controlled flat – the warden was called Linda and she had her own accommodation on the site. She was much more friendly than the previous warden and Edna loved to have a chat with her in the gardens on a sunny day. Edna still missed her old house and the neighbourhood where she and her husband, Keith, had lived for nearly 50 years. It literally was a lifetime they'd spent there.

Alison had waited for a respectable amount of time after her Dad's death before tentatively making the suggestion that her Mum should move out of the family home into something more manageable. Initially Edna resisted the idea, but she mulled it over frequently. When her elderly cleaner, Gladys, finally retired, Edna realised that she didn't like the idea of a stranger coming into her home to help her, and she couldn't bear the thought of Alison fussing around either. After Alison showed her some flats, Edna finally conceded to move into a nice place that was surrounded by a big garden with lawns and paths and somewhere to put her bird feeder.

Edna was determined to take charge in the decoration of the flat. Keith had always taken charge of the house maintenance and decoration, so Edna felt as though it had never really been hers. The new flat and the money that she'd inherited from the sale of the house gave her a happy opportunity to go on a spending spree and furnish the flat to her own taste.

Edna's life was generally a happy one, with a regular routine. Her gorgeous grandson, Petey, would pop round for tea on Tuesday evenings. They would sit together companionably at her small table, sharing the meal and chatting about his life. She would console him about his unsuccessful job-hunting exploits and make suggestions about where else he could look for opportunities. He was so sweet to her. He would often bring her a little bunch of flowers or some of the chocolates she was partial to. Edna had offered to buy him a new car (she heard

Alison moaning about the old one), but he always resisted. He always said thank you but he was happy that his old car didn't cost too much to insure and was cheap on petrol. Edna understood when Peter explained how he was actually quite fond of the car and wanted to keep it for as long as possible.

They both worried about Alison's hinting that Edna may need to move into a care home. When Edna had let the kettle burn dry on the stove, Peter had bought her an electric kettle that would switch itself off automatically. Edna pretended that she didn't see beyond Alison's "Are you OK, Mum?" questions. But she sensed a depth to the questions and responded curtly with an "I'm absolutely fine"

She'd meet her long-standing friend, Doris, a couple of times a week. There was a lovely tea shop on the High Street where they'd go and have a cup of tea and some cake, or stay for lunch, depending on the time of day. They'd been friends for longer than they could remember, but they always had things to say to each other. Doris liked Edna's slips of the tongue—saying "blow job" instead of "blow dry"—and things like that. Doris felt very maternal towards Edna and to Petey as well. She'd sympathise with Edna when Alison's fussing got too much, and she'd also express shock at the idea of putting Edna in a care home.

Alison, Peter, Edna, and Doris, each focused on their own tight aperture of the world, couldn't anticipate the change that was about to blow their perspectives wide open.

GROOVY: ZEN THOUGHTS ON WRINKLES AND MOMENTS

CELESTE REICH

Keys

As time seems to be flying by faster and faster, my desire to melt with a moment has increased tenfold. I was sitting down at my business partner's desk to do the payroll and noticed he left his keys behind in the drawer. The keys, most of them bronze in color, were worn smooth from years of handling. The desk key, the key to open the back door, the gate key and the key to the safe, all sitting there in front of me on a simple round key ring. My finger on the ridges of the keys registers how they have been worn down, proof in the silkiness that existing was real. I was immediately taken out of the present and placed into the past.

How many times over the last 30 years have these keys been used to open up that drawer to get the checkbook out and write a check? How many times at all hours of the night, was this door key put into the door to open the clinic and let a client with an emergency in? Hit by car, C-section, dog fights, wounds of all sorts, gunshot wounds, eclampsia, bloody diarrhea, urinary obstruction, foreign bodies, end stage heartworm disease, severe anemia, congestive heart failure…and all the other non-emergent calls that were emergencies in the owner's eyes? Reverse sneezing, scabies, hotspots to name a few. With each visit, the keys, doing their job, leave pieces of themselves behind in the lock hole, on the fingers of the person that worked them, and maybe even on the ground where they were thrown out of frustration from the vast amounts of turmoil that come with this job.

I especially want to emphasize that, in the past, we veterinarians used the keys to open the back door of the clinic on weekends to clean kennels, walk dogs, take care of patients, and even dig holes in the pasture to bury those who didn't make it.

I can honestly say that digging a hole while my patient lay rigid in a wheelbarrow next to me was both terrible, and a terribly important experience in my life. All the other employees would have gone home by then. There would just be me and my shovel, the wheelbarrow, and sometimes a very large dog to hoist not only into the wheelbarrow from the kennel where it took its last breath, but also to hoist out of the wheelbarrow into the hole. I can't even sort out all of the emotions I would be feeling while I wrestled with these bodies. I am just glad I had a job that meant I could experience every possible emotion a person can have, and I survived.

These experiences take their toll, making a wrinkle here either on our bodies or our minds or both. Just like the keys, we do our job and leave a piece of ourselves behind. It happens so slowly, it's barely noticeable until 20 or 30 years go by and just like the keys, we still work, but we are worn. Change is inevitable. Who knows how changes affect us? Visible or invisible. We are who we are, and we are who we have been.

Veterinary medicine molds people in strange ways as well. Some of us have a softness that is impossible to harden. Yet we find we get hard in sarcasm and a strange relationship with life as well as death and money and trying. For some of us, we wind up wanting nothing but solitude. Could it be we are afraid of being too worn, and becoming useless like a key that is broken if it gets worked too much?

It's odd that our faces get more ridges and grooves as we get old and metal grows smooth with wear. The key, already having a purpose for its whole life, was figured out at creation. When it gets worn, it loses definition, sometimes loses its purpose.

It seems we are born smooth, void of a specific purpose and as time passes, grooves start to form. Maybe, in the end, we will be some type of key, our purposeful selves a key to something else?

Could our key-self, the worn version, also be why we connect with some people and things and not with others? Is it why we get in a groove and can follow a path that takes us where we should be? The path that leads to our own predestined destination? A vocation and a soul-mate? The life that we are supposed to be living which results in peaceful acceptance of 'I am where I am supposed to be? My profession is definitely my vocation. I know I am doing what I was meant to be doing, I don't know if everyone gets to enjoy that kind of comfort in life. It seems that everything else falls into place because I am on the right path. The path was never easy and still challenging and full of good and bad but acceptance of it all comes because my key fits here.

Moments

I suspect these moments of contemplation are because I have been reading more about Zen practice in an attempt to find the purpose of life. Death is always on my mind; it has been since I was 11 years old when my brother died in a tragic accident. His death was one of those life experiences that makes a permanent groove. Like the grooves in the key, these experiences will place me in a position where I can unlock, knowingly or unknowingly, the gate to the path I am supposed to be on.

In high school I started reading books on Buddhism. The most profound teaching that I found was that the moment is all that really exists. My family went to Catholic church and always spoke of heaven and where our grandparents or our beloved dog went to after they died. That was my introduction to the afterlife. In Buddhism, there doesn't seem to be an afterlife because there is really no death, just a continuous cycle of birth and death and passing of energy into these different stages. Unless a being becomes enlightened and escapes the cycle, they continue to be. I don't know of too many moments in my life where I don't think about death. Yesterday, I euthanized four dogs in a row. It's hard to escape the thoughts of ending life in this profession, the death groove on my key-self is definitely getting worn.

On weekends I spend a lot of time at home in the barn with my horses. As I clean manure for what seems like the millionth time of the day, I pick up this particularly large ball of manure with all sorts of shavings and hay stuck to it. As I study this monstrosity on the manure fork, I am in the moment. Not in the past, not in the future but right here and now. I am struck with the realization that we are actually living in the afterlife and it is amazing.

In my naive life experience, I've only been taught of the after-life being heaven, where everything is perfect and something that happens after life is over. In Zen practice, there isn't the same idea of the afterlife as most of us know it. I am not expert by any means but in Zen, now is all that exists, nothing else matters. When we are awake to that knowledge, it is heavenly. So, the construct of my key self that has been developed thus far with my life experiences has created this idea of the "afterlife" as my own Zen mind might see it. The moment after the moment which is always right here and right now. Still staring at the manure fork, I contemplate the sticky ball of poop, and see that our lives are a shit ball full of everything we just went through in previous moments. We should observe it for what it is and toss it away just the same as I toss the poop ball into the wheelbar-row. All the good and all the bad equally disposed. This concept seems to allow me to cope better with the daily struggles and ups and downs of a profession where one often has to decide between something so material as money and something so sacred as life. If I allow myself to flow with thoughts coming and going rather than mulling over and grabbing onto the particularly bad ones, I seem to be able to get better sleep at night.

Shunryu Suzuki, a Japanese Zen priest and the author of Zen Mind, Beginner's Mind says to "'Leave your front door and your back door open. Allow your thoughts to come and go. Just don't serve them tea."

The poop ball made me realize we don't hang on to our own body waste. We don't cling to it like we do all our own ideas and definitions of ourselves and our judgements of others. Good or bad, we can let these things move on and try to check out the next moment free of our "I".

The idea behind Zen practice involves focusing on the here and now without thinking, just being present. If I can inhabit my Zen practice like I intend to do, every moment dies and no longer exists. The future does not exist. The right here and now is all that exists. Since this moment is after the last moment died, what we are experiencing is the birth of a new moment. Realizing this quality of every one of our present moments makes it hard to not to be joyful.

I am learning to believe that what matters is not where we have been or where we are going, but the tiny simple moment that we (or at least I) tend to forget, which is right now. Of course, my attempt to explain my approach to Zen mind with conscious effort, completely contradicts the whole idea of Zen practice. It's not possible to verbalize this ultimate state of reality.

Suzuki also says "As soon as you see something, you already start to intellectualize it. As soon as you intellectualize something, it is no longer what you saw."

I pair Suzuki's idea about intellectualizing with author Paulo Coehlo's ideas from his novel, The Alchemist: "When you want something, all the universe conspires in helping you to achieve it." I feel like Cohelo's idea goes along Zen practice. Not that there is "want" or even "I" in Zen practice, but when people are in tune with every moment to their fullest, things easily happen, in the way they should happen, almost as if we are where we should be in the universe. By placing ourselves in the now, we are "right" with the universe for this moment in time, so everything flows without a hitch.

As I think about the keys and their worn metal and their function and purpose, I think about myself. How experience and education and hardships and happy times have shaped me. I am a key in production. One day I will stop thinking and just work, like the keys to those doors, drawers, and gates. No thought, just action. In the beginning of my career, I would lay awake at night worrying, stressing, thinking way too much. Retaining all the shit from the day, bigger than that poop ball on the manure fork, thinking and rethinking, unable to stop the thoughts until the wee hours of the morning and then have to experience another day to add to my already weary mind. The shaping of my key-self in overdrive. I can't see where it happened, but I became an expert at throwing thoughts away and letting them go, learning to accept that I will do the best I can and focus on the moments. Had I not developed this ability, it's possible my key would have broken, leading me way off my path.

Sometimes this all goes way over my head, and other times I feel like I am bobbing along with it at the surface. Here's to always being present and open, to feeling rather than thinking, to compassion paired with kindness, and to following our hearts. Life is way too short to let any of it go without recognition.

SHAME QUARANTINE

SUSAN HANNAH HULL

My protector, it keeps me safe . . .
not happy, but safe is what matters!

Stay home, it urges.
Nobody will tell you to go home if you
are already there. (And be sure nobody
comes to the door.)

Nobody can see all the ways
you're so flawed, so not perfect,
if you don't go where they might sense
what's going on inside.
Oh, and then
they can't see the outside either,
all the bumps and wrinkles.

Maybe I'll just go out for a little while,
It might be fun . . .
But is it worth the risk?

I'll wear a mask! One that covers my nose and mouth,
so I can't really breathe but they won't smell

my bad breath.
And I can't really speak but it will be
carefully filtered,
so they won't hear that I don't know
what I'm talking about.

God it hurts so much when I fall
into this pit of shame.

But I sure do know my way around, and
it's so safe here . . . but wait, a tendril of a thought pushes
through the edge of my brain.

Just a thought…what if it isn't true
that something so bad will happen that I shouldn't even try?

My protector hurries to remind me: Something might happen!
Yes, I say, something definitely will happen.
and I think, just maybe, I want to live with it.

JOURNEY OF A SACRED PASSAGE DOULA

AMANDA JANE LARAMORE

The sun beat down on us, horses and people gathered for summer clinics and riding. We were mesmerized by the clinicians. Dust rose around us as and covered weathered leather chaps and jeans. The anticipation of this clinic was finally a reality and our energy was high, lighthearted and hopeful. My mind was as far away from my worries as it could be.

I received the phone call in the afternoon: "Amanda, your Mom has not gotten out of bed all day." I knew that things had changed, and a fear and unease overcame me.

Mom had been moved in the last week to an in-home care facility. two blocks from my home. She was the only resident at the time, receiving Kay's focused care and companionship that left me feeling safe and calm enough to attend a horse clinic. The peace evaporated as I left the clinic and drove directly to see Mom to assess the situation for myself.

I walked into her room and laid eyes on her. Having companioned many people as they transitioned in the last days of their lives, as a soul midwife, the feel in the room was clear and instinct gnawed. My gut knew that she had made a huge shift in her state of awareness. My mom was beginning the process of her ascension and separating from this plane. The previous day, and historically, my mother was ambulatory, animated, and agitated at times. Most days she walked and paced for up to twelve hours. This day, her primary motor cortex no longer made connection, debilitating her limbs and taking away her ability to walk. Pale, she no longer wanted to eat or drink. My mother spent time venturing behind the veil.

For her 73 years physically present on earth my mom was called Naomi. She was a South African-raised woman. She appeared to be a gorgeous, 55-year-old lady with blonde hair and blue eyes. People often remarked at her youthfulness and beauty. Alzheimer's disease had begun to change her perception, cognition, and emotionality, beginning in her late 50s. My mother was a fiercely proud and private woman who did not find her voice in her adult life.

Knowing that my dear Mom was in her final days, I prayed and hoped for her to be able to genuinely express herself and to overcome those things that bound and tormented her. I visualized and summoned a herd of white horses to accompany her, empowering her as she detached from this world. I recall an image of a print I had on my dresser, of a white Pegasus that spoke to me. I visualized the Pegasus coming to be with my mom. My three brothers, and their families came to visit Mom and say their goodbyes. We spent beautiful moments in vigil for the woman who cared for us and birthed us. This unfolding and letting go went into its 5th week. I was beginning to memorize the words to all of her favorite songs. "It won't be easy, you'll think it strange, When I try to explain how I feel, that I still need your love after all that I've done."

I took my Father to say good-bye to his wife of 50 years, on Friday morning, August 5th. Naomi was less responsive: her breathing was interrupted, while her body was weak and laboring. Nora, my new granddaughter and keeper of my heart, nestled in her Mom's arms on the couch across from the bed, and my attention was on their loveliness. I turned my gaze to the bed and held my breath. I watched. Nothing. Mom's breathing had ceased, and she presented with no movement in her chest and no heartbeat. I walked over to her, taking her vitals, and finding no response. My dear mother had crossed over. I let out a cry, "Mamma."

There were two hospice nurses in the kitchen at Walden Place. I asked for them to please come and assist us. One of the nurses entered the room, checking for a pulse and respirations before affirming that Mom was dead. She left to get her stethoscope and summon the other hospice nurse who would call time of death. While the nurse was checking Mom's heart rate one last time, my mother took a breath and looked at us. All of us were in awe of what we had witnessed. My mom crossed over and spent about five minutes in the light, only to return.

There must have been something unresolved for my Mom. What? I didn't understand what could be keeping her. All of her children, and husband had come by to say adieu. I received a phone call from a friend, Megan Powers, a Gestalt Equine Institute of the Rockies counselor and shaman, who was checking in with me on August 7th. She had just lost her father and was offering her love and support. I hesitantly shared the story of Mom's death and resurfacing. Megan offered her guidance and came to visit my Mom the following day. Megan spent several hours alone with my Mom. Together they entered a shamanic-soul journey. At that time Mom was virtually not responsive to verbal communication, and she had stable vital signs.

After working with Mom, Megan shared with us that Naomi's spirit guide immediately showed up in her mind's eye in the form of a White Pegasus. Speechless, with goosebumps we listened intently to Megan's story of how Naomi showed up to do her work. She resolved generational imprints of blame and shame, releasing the ties that burdened her. Naomi battled her demons, let go of the intergenerational patterns, and reclaimed her power. My Mom spoke her truth. That evening some friends and I spent time with Mom, as she rested. We drank wine and I shared the astounding details of her shamanic journey. I brought the picture of the white Pegasus to her room and placed it on the bedroom dresser intentionally facing it towards her. Kay promised she would call if anything changed and, at midnight I returned home. I had confidence that naturally several physical unfoldings needed to occur for Mom to die. Her heart rate and respirations were far from someone in their final hours.

At 3:40 a.m. Kay called to tell me that, while Kay had been in the bathroom, my precious Mom had died. The white Pegasus accompanied my Naomi, and her herd on the breath of dawn, soaring to the light of a distant star. I drove to Walden House, climbed into bed with Mom, and I snuggled myself under the covers with the baby doll she held in arms.

Was this really it.? Yes, my Mamma had really left her earthly body. The room that once was filled with angelic guides was empty. My Mom was really gone. She let go. She let go on her 74th birthday, almost at exactly the same time that she was born, in Cape Town, in her grandparents' farmhouse. Full circle. Choice. Despite her cognitive disabilities, her soul maintained its intention and path. I stayed in the bed with her for hours soaking up every bit of her warmth and smell, taking every bit of her in. I chanted Mommy, Mommy, Mommy. Phil and I assisted in bathing, dressing, and accompanying my Mom to the Funeral Home's removal van hours later.

My husband asked if I wanted a ride home. I chose to walk. My legs were weighted, my breath slow, my limbs extended as the Banyan trees roots system, deep into the earth. I was present, I was peaceful. I was vulnerable. I was home. I questioned my mindset, as this was such an unusual state of physical and emotional feeling and response to losing my mother.

Several months later at another class offered by the horse clinician, we practiced a grounding exercise. With eyes closed we circled in different directions, bringing the circle inward more and more, then dropping our energy back to the center of the earth. Mark asked us to open our eyes and then walk when we were ready. This grounding exercise took me back to the day I walked home alone after my Mother had died. Overtaken with emotion, I shared the story and the brilliance of how I felt at that present moment after completing the exercise: grounded, whole, present, and full of profound peace. I was beginning to understand. The feeling that we seek to achieve in softness and connection with our horses was offered to me as my Mom shared the joy of her state of being in ascension. Her gift to me was continuing to seek out this space of joy and connection with myself and my horse. The perfect synchronicity, congruence, being, and letting go that Mark described made sense.

My journey with horses is in the infancy stage. My husband suggested equine therapy after a brief trail ride the previous winter. Conflicted I was longing to hold presence with beautiful horses was undeniable even while my fear was palpable. In the unfolding I found Happy Dog Ranch, and eventually adopted one of the horses, a chestnut Arabian gelding, Sundancer.

We spent a lot of time in Crested Butte. There was a horse, Ghost, with whom I spent time trail riding. The connection and closeness I felt with him was uncanny, a homecoming, if you will. We understood one another and bonded. When he was wintered in Almont, my husband and I would stop and see him, making me cry with joy. I have photos of him in my home. He would visit in my waking and in my sleeping. In the fall of September 2018, we were celebrating our wedding anniversary and I scheduled a ride with Ghost. Ghost was for sale; the decision was made instantaneously to provide him a shelter with us. Ghost is now a part of our herd. Our earthly white Pegasus is home.

I am growing, evolving, and finding my true self in the presence of my equi-partners. The depth and breadth of joy and peace I find in the company of horses, when we listen deeply with intent and partnership, is like nothing else. In gratitude with mindful breath we go and be together.

Naomi, you are felt on the breath of horses in the early morning frost. I feel you in the golden sunshine on bluebird sky days. I feel you in the changing of the leaves. I feel you as the crisp cold contacts my cheeks. You shared with me the greatest gift in your final days. I listened. I listened to you. In the silent stillness, I listened and felt the joy and connection and the eternal. I strive, daily, to bring this same softness and relationship with presence, to my growing connectedness to Sundancer and Ghost Soul-Shine. Listen to the horse. I have learned that my heart will be filled with an expansive love and shared connected consciousness with the sentient horse.

A FALL IN THREE STATES

CRISSI MCDONALD

An Afternoon Walk Through New Hampshire Woods

I don't know
the names of trees nor the bird voices that
sing out
unseen.
I don't know (but I do now)
what the irregular woody thumps are
behind me
(I'm being stalked by falling acorns).
I don't know the scent of these
Ginger cinnamon eucalyptus woods
as my feet cicada scuffle through
red and
yellow and
brown fallen leaves.
I don't know the sight of sunlight through
these deciduous and temperamental
eastern trees.
But I do know,
as in Nature,
I am a part of the whole woods
and the birds

and the stalking acorns that
squirrels gather for their
cold winter days.

A Walk in Maryland Woods, Evening

The trees of these woods
still hang on to green.
Pinking rays of sunset slanting through
their trunks.
The dogs scatter undergrowth and
there are iridescent green small things (ferns, trees?)
growing in clusters,
huddling their pliable bodies in a community.
I avoid stepping on them.
The dogs race on, chasing through vines and grasses
panting in counterpoint to
cricket song.
The dogs chase on, seeing rabbits in ferns
and birds singing to the skies.

Morning, An Iowa Pond

Here, there are
five different bird songs,
bursts of arpeggios
a ululation
an exaltation that
births the morning
bright and brilliant as
the trees that adorn themselves
in wardrobes of orange and yellow.
A fallen tree melts into earth.
Surrounded by this beauty,
I could do the same.

NAN AND GRANDAD HOW—A STEP BACK IN TIME

SUE HILL

Nan and Grandad lived in West Ham, in northeast London. We lived in a new town, about thirty-five miles north of London and any expedition to visit them involved great planning and car checking and the rounding up of children (I am one of five), so it only happened once or twice a year.

Their house was one in a line of terraced houses with a narrow frontage—the front door was on the left and a bay window to the right. There were two tall, thin windows upstairs.

Their road was a "cul-de-sac" which ended in a small curve. Nan would take us through a walkway there on the way to the nearest underground station (which was, perversely, over ground on that section of the line)

There was no front garden, but there was a small concreted area and a low wall separating the house from the road. Dad would park in the road outside the house—parking was no problem back then. We'd bundle out with relief and excitement after the long journey and race each other to the front door, which was never locked, and thunder down the long, dark corridor to the back of the house, shattering the peace that Nan and Grandad would have been enjoying.

The corridor was dark and narrow and seemed to go on forever. It smelled dark—it wasn't an unclean smell, but just smelled old. Entering the corridor from the outside was like entering a cool, dark cave. The floor was covered in a light brown linoleum on top of a springy wooden floor which answered our enthusiastic steps with creaks and sighs. The ceiling was high, much higher than the ceilings in our modern house, yet the hallway felt claustrophobic. There were two doors leading to living rooms to the right of the corridor and to the left, there was a large, dark brown piece of hall furniture that housed many coats and hats. Theirs was a hat-wearing generation, and Grandad's flat cap would be uppermost. The two rooms to the right of the corridor were linked with a handy sliding partition. The front room was full of Grandad's gardening trophies. He had an allotment a couple of miles away, and spent many happy days successfully cultivating prize-winning fruits and vegetables. We'd sometimes call in there on the way to Nan and Grandad's and my siblings and I would gather around his raspberry canes to feast like a flock of hungry blackbirds.

The second room was rarely used, but I do remember sleeping in there once when staying with Nan and Grandad. My cousin Bobby was staying too, and he slept in the front room. We were chattering through the partition after dark, and he sang the Beatles song "When I'm Sixty-Four" to me, until the noise got to Nan and she'd bellow from upstairs "will you be quiet!" which would shush us into a muffled giggling silence.

At the end of the corridor was the staircase leading up to two bedrooms—deep, wooden steps, is how I remember them—and the corridor turned sharp right, down a step, and then sharp left and into the parlour. Just before the door to the parlour, on the left, was a large cupboard built into the space under the stairs. It seemed to go from floor to ceiling and had large wooden doors with recessed panels. The paintwork was a creamy yellow and the shelves were dark, bare wood. This was the cupboard where Nan kept an abundance of treats for sticky-fingered children.

On the right was a door to Hades. Well . . . not Hades, but the cellar. Through the cellar door were some old rickety wooden steps leading into complete darkness. We were told that there were rats "down there," so we were never tempted to go further than sticking our noses into the gloom beyond the top step. I'm not sure if the rat story was true, or just a way to scare small people away from the danger of the steep stairs. Either way, it was effective.

Stepping into the parlour, we reached a haven of light and warmth and comfort—like climbing into someone's lap for a big cuddle. Nan and Grandad lived in this room. It had a real fire, two big, squishy, very old armchairs that would give up the secrets of their previous occupants as you nestled into their snugness. A wooden table on the right, underneath a nylon-netted window was the place where Nan and Grandad ate. I have a clear memory of Grandad standing at the table, carving bread and butter for tea. He would grip the loaf of bread, apply butter to the open end of it, then carve the buttered slice from the loaf, still held in his hand. The feat showed amazing precision and resulted in a paper thin and superbly neat slice. I found it hypnotizing to watch. I've tried many times to emulate his method but have never come close to achieving his beautiful precision.

At the back of the parlour, the floor and the wall had had a disagreement, and the floor gaped away leaving a long gap suggesting another entrance to Hades. When I was older and asked Mum why the landlord had let them live in such bad conditions, she explained that they paid an extremely low rent in return for accepting the house as it was.

Beyond the parlour was the last room in the house—referred to as the scullery. It wasn't well equipped enough to be called a kitchen. It was dark, despite the window leading to the back garden, and seemed to only be used for cooking on the stove. There was a large stoneware sink and a bare wooden draining board set beneath the window. A door to the right led out into the small garden.

This was the way out to the "privy"—the outside toilet. It was an adventure to answer one's needs at Nanny and Grandad's house. The loo was at the rear of the property, built into the back of the house. It had a wooden door, roughly fit to give just enough privacy. The loo smelled clean and the loo paper was usually the papery kind found in schools—I seem to remember the brand name "Izal," probably a foreign word for "non-absorbent" or "slippery." It always felt a little adventurous to leave the house without an adult's direct supervision. When we stayed overnight, a chamber pot was placed under the bed for night-time needs. I found myself markedly continent when staying there. The thought of "performing" into a pot and having my output sit there for all to see was unbearable.

The little garden was overgrown with long grass and bushes. In the back of the garden was an Anderson Shelter—a structure made with corrugated iron sheets, dug down into the ground to provide some protection from bombs during World War Two. It's hard to imagine how a covering of corrugated iron would provide protection from such a rude invasion of privacy. This one was barely visible through the undergrowth, and was partially collapsed, but it was a sight of morbid curiosity for me. I always felt slightly uncomfortable—whether it was the ghosts hinted at by the shelter, the various monsters lurking in the untamed undergrowth, or the fact that people had really had to try and shelter from the horror of bombs in such a flimsy and inadequate structure, I'm not sure.

Back in the house, Grandad would have "put the kettle on" to make tea. It was always tea in Nan and Grandad's house. The fire would be blazing because, regardless of the season, Nan felt the cold. Nan would be cossetted in one of the comfy armchairs and would welcome smaller children into her lap for a cuddle. She had a cheeky smile and twinkly eyes and short, gleaming white hair. She always wore an apron—usually patterned with small colourful flowers.

Nan was born in 1900. She was short and wide. For people

who know me, I've inherited her conformation. I've also inherited her short snub nose and an almost insatiable thirst for sugar. Nan was diabetic towards the end of her life (I'm doing my best to avoid that) but she would still sneak sugary treats like a naughty schoolgirl. She would also enjoy her sugar vicariously by feeding her many grandchildren with unhealthy but desirable treats. The cupboard outside the parlour door was always full of chocolates, sweets and biscuits, which were freely distributed. To Mother's frequently voiced frustration, she would even serve us oranges cut in half with a sugar cube pressed down into the centre. Nan's drink of choice, after tea, was cream soda—a sticky, sweet beverage which even now makes me gag at the memory of the taste. Nan was happy to pander to the foibles of her grandchildren. My sister Kay retained a penchant for Farley's Rusks—a baby food—well into her older childhood and Nan would make sure she had some in the cupboard whenever we visited.

Nan loved taking her younger charges into central London when they came to stay. Her favourite place was Trafalgar Square, populated then and now by hundreds of pigeons. Street hawkers would sell little pots of grain which she would buy for us so that we could feed the birds. In fact, if you're familiar with the original Mary Poppins film, there's a scene where an old lady sat on the steps of St. Paul's Cathedral during the song "Feed the Birds"—she could have been my Nan. I cry happy tears at the memory of her at that point in the film.

We would travel into town on the underground—Nan would keep us amused by fishing around in her Mary Poppins handbag for "Murray Mints"—the supply never, ever dried up. To a child, it seemed miraculous. The journey was an adventure for us "out of towners." Nan would always fall asleep, and we would grow more and more anxious because we were never sure which of the myriad of stops would be ours. We fidgeted, wavering between risking her wrath by waking her, or suffering the life-ending tragedy of missing our stop. Without fail, she would magically wake up just as we reached our stop, gather us up and depart the train with cool confidence.

It's over 40 years since Nan & Grandad passed away. As I am now a Grandparent (a Nana) myself, I have a wonderful appreciation of how special the relationship between Grandparent and Grandchild can be. I am very grateful that my life overlapped with my Grandparents long enough for them to leave such lasting memories in my heart and mind. I hope that these memories will bring Nan and Grandad to life for you.

FUNERAL INTERRUPTED

PATTI BREHLER

I beat my feet beneath the burning sun,
among the trees to find some sweet relief,
yet nothing freed me as I came undone—
how far must one run to bury one's grief?
I interrupted a funeral of geese
guarding a lifeless lump of yellow down;
wings flailed as their desperate honks increased—
I ached to submerge in the lake and drown.
I saw two men in suits at father's door,
holding time until our goodbyes we cried;
hands clasped over groins awaiting their chore,
as if to protect from the grief inside.
Geese winged away to return to their clan.
Men took his body and I ran and ran.

THE FLIES

JOANNA SAVAGE COLEMAN

They say if you stand out on the cliffs at four in the afternoon, with a brass compass pointed due west, and carry in your pocket a swatch of your grandmother's wedding-dress – maybe from her second or third wedding – that you can see the edge of the world.

I came out here often, leaving the bitumen of the Old Town behind and following the goat-track as it twists and bucks under my bicycle tires. The undergrowth is thick and wind hardened. The bushes are bunched and gnarled around themselves as though knotted by the salty air. They say the water below the cliffs is littered with the bodies of desperate factory workers who plunged to the next life after the cannery closed down. Some say they didn't really die. Some say they stay locked down there, just below the surface. Like fingerprints trapped under glass, looking up at those of us who stand on the edge above them. Just waiting.

It was April when the flies came. They began in the corners of my eyes, then fled from my swatting fingers to multiply in the unseen places of my home while I was distracted. They moved from the bedroom with me when I woke and followed me to the shower where I shaved my face clean.

They joined me for breakfast. Hunched over at the sink, milk trickling down my arm. They crawled along my knuckles as I read the news. They harassed sweat from my pores, making themselves a watering-hole of my skin.

Soon the flies seemed to be more inside than outside. I never mentioned them, and neither did anyone else. It was as though they had always been here. Best not to draw attention to them. I rode to the corner-store for milk and cigarettes. The flies watched me, hung silent on the windowpanes. People say cigarettes cost an arm and a leg once. Maybe that was before they wanted us to die.

They say the Old Town was a happy place once. A place for young couples to start families, go to church, play ballgames in the park after work. I rode home alone, the flies pinned wet to my hairline. I found myself opening my door carefully so as not to let them out. Whether I wished to keep them from the world, or keep them to myself, I couldn't be sure. I scoured each chipped and flaking windowsill for their expired bodies, but I never found one. They didn't die here.

I liked the flies. I had to. They blanketed every facet of my life and brought my attention to things I had never noticed before; the way the sunlight drifted through the curtains on a warm day, the way I left the jam out with the lid off overnight. The grooves under the toilet seat from which they sheepishly crawled when I turned on the light. The damp corners of my eyes. The loose seal my lips formed around my cigarette, allowing them to enter and exit my mouth as they pleased.

I started talking to them. Just a word here and there to begin with. Whispers of indignation. Go away you little blighters. A greeting in the morning. Or a goodnight as I fell into bed. Reflexive things. The kind of things you come to do when you are alone. Like talking to a photograph. It didn't mean anything. That's what I told myself. But then I dreamt of them. Twisted and gnarled together, sculpted into human form so as to put me at ease.

That was the first time we kissed earnestly. Passionately. The flies entering and exiting my lips at will. But this time I wanted them. We embraced long into the early hours of the morning. When I woke my lover was scattered about my walls and windows, appearing again as hundreds of crawling insects. Our little secret, I smiled. She was shy. Best not to draw attention to her.

I talked to her about my life, my fears, my secrets. I told her the legends of the Old Town. How if you were to walk over the concreted-up well in the centre, the temperature of your body would drop six degrees and you would hear the voices of the women who were drowned there. I told her about how I had come to be here. How I had come to be alone. How none of it had been my fault and that I felt numbness where I should have felt sensations of guilt. She watched me and listened; an audience of soft black eyes and slowly moving legs. Are you washing or are you praying? I asked. No reply. Just a knowing smile. The gentle kiss of wings on my cheek. The comfort of soft humming. The whisper of saccharine nothings deep inside my ear canals; a language only I could understand.

I would miss them if they were gone. The company through the days and passions in my sleep. They joined me in everything I did. They saw every inch of me, even the things I'd seek to hide from others. Every smell, every liquid. They worshipped me, and I satiated them. I began to agonise over their passing. What if one day I woke up and they were gone? I didn't sleep. I stayed up into the early hours talking to them where they gathered on my bedspread, unaffected by the coming cold. I told them everything. Every secret, every shame, every regret. They listened and they watched me, but I could offer them so little in thanks for their companionship.

As the winter formed and woke, they began to disappear. Just one here, two there. Gone from my mirror as I shaved my face. Gone from the walls in the hall as I walked to breakfast. One in the jam jar. What can I do? What can I do for you to have you stay with me? They were silent. Watching and listening as I ate over the sink. My heart ached and I could no longer feel the warm sensation of hundreds of tiny feet massaging its rhythm.

They say if you stand out on the cliffs at four in the afternoon with a brass compass pointed due west. They say if you keep in your pocket a swatch of the wedding dress worn by your grandmother on her second or third wedding. They say if you do this, and your heart is pure, that you can see the edge of the world.

I've been here many times before. Up the goat-track on my bicycle. The underbrush is thick, and you could hide things here that no one else would ever find. Secrets. The hum of the flies grows louder, and she forms from the air beside me. Beautiful and black and shining. Glittering with hundreds of delicate, velvet-kissed exoskeletons. Her skin writhes and pulses. I look out towards the horizon, ashamed to rest my eyes on her. She watches me and listens.

If she spoke, she would take me back to the apartment in the city, asking me again why I would want to move to the Old Town anyway. Ask me what is so special about a town that's been forgotten. She'd ask me why I don't want her to speak with her family anymore. Why I get angry over the smallest things. She'd ask me why I would bring her so far away from everything, then leave her alone out here. Buried under the salt-gnarled underbrush.

But she says nothing. She is silent. The humming stills and she dissipates, broken apart and leaving me alone on the cliff. I turn and face due west, the setting sun burning warm on my stubbled jaw. I fondle the scrap of Grandmother's dress in my pocket. I think of my young wife and I tell her I'm sorry. I wait. The souls of the canners look up at me, laughing from beneath their glass prison. I can't see the edge of the world. I can't see anything at all.

VOICES OF SHE

It took me quite a long time to develop a voice, and now that I have it, I am not going to be silenced.

Madeleine Albright

WOMEN IN LITERARY DESIRE

MARY MCGINNIS

We must unpack our doubts, believe
in ourselves, shedding nightmare
masks—because
every one of us is more than a
number, more than an
inflated ego, more than
nausea following chemo, more than
lumps, more than
inevitably thinning hair.
We touch our deepest memories,
each one changing, becoming slightly
rumpled but real.
At last, young and old
dreams mixing, discovering
each day a
silence we will share from
inside to paper, the
raw, the relived:
precious and precise.

THE END OF THE STORY

PAULA ROMANOW

The dusty bone-china cup and saucer had sat on Anya's kitchen shelf forever, it seemed. They had travelled with her from rooms to apartments to houses, relics of her many moves during her student days and young adulthood, through a marriage and its ending to now. "Now" wasn't a very good place to be. Now was barely fifty, alone, broke and dying. She looked around her emptied living room. The truck from the charity would be here shortly, and there was still a lot to do. How to reduce a lifetime's memories into one box, one room in a hospice? She sighed. Soon enough it wouldn't matter.

Anya placed the cup and saucer in the donation box. Then, inexplicably, she took them out again and returned them to the shelf. They were all she had to remind her of the days when she had still believed that life was fair, that it would last forever. Looking back, she remembered where the set had come from; her grandmother, an inveterate collector of bone-china. It represented a gentility that her grandmother had believed was superior to the farm she'd been brought up on. The cup and saucer would remind Anya of her roots, her grandmother had said when she gave it to her. It was the day Anya had left home for university, the first woman in her family not to marry while still in high school. Those roots were long gone. Her family had never understood her life or her need to be her own person.

One by one, they'd drifted away, gently or violently, depending on their temperament, and the strength of their religious beliefs.

Next to the cup and saucer was a photo of her and Joel. She wasn't sure why she'd kept it after he left her. Probably because she'd stopped seeing it there, just as he'd stopped seeing her not long after their tenth anniversary.

Anya remembered the day the photo had been taken. They'd put a good face on it for their friend Esther, who'd come to dinner to celebrate Joel's successful show opening. Esther couldn't feel the cracks, or see the greyness surrounding them. But they could. Anya could see it in their eyes, in the stiff way they held themselves in the photo. Touching Joel was almost more than she could bear, but Esther insisted, chivvying them along into some semblance of joy. Which was ironic, because Joel had just revealed that he was leaving Anya for Joy Watters, a woman twice her age and still younger than him, although not by much. He was bored, although that wasn't the excuse he gave. Anya had been his model and his lover for too long not to feel the slow seeping away of his attention. How she came to regret the hours she'd spent listening to his overtold stories, laughing at his jokes, and feeling his despair during his creative process. He'd always said she was his muse when he was feeling good about his latest painting. But as the opening grew nearer, it began to appear that he didn't need his muse, or at least not her version of it, anymore. Now, creation done, he'd moved on.

Still, he'd given her a good settlement, and the pain and humiliation eventually faded. He'd been a poor substitute for her family anyway. Esther hadn't hung around for long either. A former muse of a famous man just didn't have the same cachet, she supposed. Shaking her head, Anya removed the photo from the frame and slowly tore it up. The frame went into the donation box and stayed there.

Looking around her, she suddenly needed to shake the heaviness of the past, and the future, off her shoulders. There was nothing for her here, no one left to care about her things, her will was in order, and frankly, soon it wouldn't be her problem anyway. Grabbing her jacket and her pills, she didn't bother locking the door behind her.

She stopped short when she got outside. Everything had a super-charged haze, seemed so real all of a sudden, that it was almost painful. She needed to orient herself. The glare of the sun, the traffic noise, the claustrophobic feeling of buildings rising high in every direction, the people rushing past her, left her overwhelmed, buffeted by the life around her. Anya turned left, instinctively moving down the street to the one safe space left in the city. Two blocks down, which was about all she could manage any more, was a pocket park, tucked in between two apartment buildings. A reminder of her grandmother's farm: peaceful and hidden from sight. Taking the path between the autumn maples, she found her favourite bench.

Then, emptying her mind, she let the green embrace her, and stepped into her future.

This piece is from an in-progress novel.

ARE YOU IN THERE?

ALYSSA REVELS

Are you in there?
Soft, stretched skin
Dark, coarse hairs
Marching single file along that linea negra
From my belly button south.
My fingers trace that pliable space—
Not long vacated by another.
A mirrored reflection.
A steamy moment of both hope and worry.
Are you in there?
Is my body my own?
Or do I already share my sacred space
With someone new?
Unknown.
Unmet.
Are you in there?

THIEVERY

ABBY LETTERI

When we get caught, it goes like this.

Marie carries the donkey bag on her left shoulder. You know what a donkey bag is, right? A sack-like cloth purse made from some block-printed fabric, Mexican or Indian, with embroidery and maybe some tassels. Holds a lot.

Marie is tall and startlingly beautiful, a teenaged Botticelli's Venus. Everyone's a bit in awe, and nobody messes with her. She flicks off compliments like bits of confetti, adoration like sea spray. Her words, when she uses them, have flinty edges. She is the original chestnut mare.

We go to the five and dime exactly as we have so many times before. We browse together, then we split up. Many little things, inconsequential things, slip into the bag. Nothing important, certainly nothing we need, as if that is even the point. Eventually I make my way to the checkout and Marie joins me in line. I buy a little something — a small notebook, a tiny pen with turquoise ink — and we saunter out of the store and into the hot sun.

Every nerve in our bodies sizzles with the electric thrill.

Every time we get away with it, it goes just like this: we keep up our languid stroll, the brash cool of it, shoulders squared, carrying our heads like Egyptian goddesses … until we turn the corner and duck into the familiar maze of alleys that lead back to our block. There, out of view, we suck in breath, gulp air, blow out raucous laughter. We adore ourselves and each other, revel in our wicked, glorious joy.

Back home, we dump the loot on Marie's bed. A jumble of useless plastic objects spilling onto the duvet. Lipsticks we will never wear, a pearl-colored French barrette, a miniature sewing kit in a little plastic suitcase and, once, a pack of ACE playing cards featuring an antique steam train.

Oh, we are good!

Until the day the manager is waiting for us just outside. He turns us back through the front door, the bell jingling above our heads and marches us to his office at the back of the store. In the hallway, he grabs Marie by her long, copper braid and hauls her up against the wall next to the cheap plastic frame announcing the Employee of the Month (Blanche, July 1971). The manager's face is the color of a boiled beet.

I'm choking back tears, but Marie's face is stony as a Greek statue. Wisps of copper where curls have come loose from the braid float around her pale, freckled face. The manager spills the contents of the donkey bag onto his desk and glares at Marie. He calls the police and then we wait. For what seems like eternity.

By the time the plain-clothed officer arrives, the manager has gone somewhere "to cool off" and left us in the custody of the junior manager. He is a youth, not much older than us, weedy, beak-nosed, with a tick in his right eye and unfortunate short pants. Grubby white socks. I feel like I am hallucinating.

The officer and the junior manager exchange pleasantries and we are led back out to the front of the store. The junior manager points to the pipe in the officer's vest pocket and asks him his brand of choice. Selects a packet and hands it over. The officer turns and looks Marie directly in the eyes. Does he wink? He says, "OK, girls. I'm taking you home."

I am aware that I am completely invisible.

The dispatch radio in the unmarked squad car is crackling and barking from somewhere under the dashboard. Dionne Warwick on the car radio, Walk on By. The officer switches it off and takes a notebook from his pocket. Asks our names. Ages. Parents' names. Addresses. Writes it all down carefully and when he's done, he rips out the page, folds it in half and puts it in his breast pocket with the tobacco and pipe.

A block before Marie's house, the officer pulls over and tells us to get out. "Go home," he says, "and be cool. Wouldn't want to upset your parents, seeing you in a car with a strange man."

Speechless, we climb out and walk unsteadily away. He toots the horn. We turn. He's taken the folded page from his pocket and is holding it out the window, tearing it into shreds. They fall from his fingers like tiny blossoms.

HOW TO BE

LOUISE THAYER

Re-borne
into this world
on the wings of angels,
(white feathers flying).

When you can,
(not now),
you will
re-enter the body
you fight still
to stay outside.

The first time your spirit left
was (most likely)
the first time you knew love
and felt loss so great
it unearthed you.

How?

(come back)

To this suit of skin?

Like gloves made of hide
a size too big
and worn too thin.

Not now
(but later),
when you can.

Fly in
on white wings
or slip in
singing.

Burst
with unchecked laughter.

You might at first
feel the shock
of expelling
after holding your breath for

so long.

It doesn't mean that they're gone.

You are welcome.

You are home.

AUNT BOBBIE'S PLACE

KIMBERLY GRIFFIN

I was ten years old, almost, and I couldn't sleep. All I could do was kick my feet under the sheets in my wee bed, like Roadrunner in the cartoons, and squeal into my pillow. In the morning I was going to Aunt Bobbie's and Uncle Walt's ranch!

I got to spend two weeks there, without my parents, but my younger sister also got to come. She always got to come. We would have this opportunity for several years, every summer. For me, it was better than my birthday, or Christmas, even Halloween, and I really liked dressing in costumes.

My parents decided that, rather than drive us from Los Angeles to Phoenix, we were old enough to fly. So, I arrived at LAX wearing my best dress. I hated dresses, but this was not an issue worth fighting about, crinoline, white socks with lace tops rolled down, and black patent leather Mary-Janes. I even had the requisite little white gloves on my clenched fists and a ribbon in hair. It was 1963.

Once free of our parents and sans ribbon, I tucked the arch strap of my shoes back to the heel, for a more grown up image, and managed to lose the gloves.

I settled into my very first airplane ride. My sister had the window, it was just easier that way.

We had a layover in Denver, I think. Since I was the oldest, the stewardess spoke with me about where the hands of the clock should be when it was time to board the next plane. She deposited my sister and me on chairs in front of said clock to wait. And wait we did. I never took my eyes off that clock. I could tell time but did not want to risk missing the most important destination of my life--Aunt Bobbie, the desert, and horses.

I was born in Phoenix, and my parents had a small place with two corrals just across the road from the gymkhana clubhouse and grounds, complete with arena, judging box, and grandstands. I would later have the opportunity to compete in horseback races with an egg held in a spoon and another where everyone's boots are in a pile at the end of the arena. We would race down, find a pair, remount, and race back.

One day I was sitting in the grandstands all alone, a dust storm was brewing and had sent a wee dust devil that danced across the arena. I thought it would be fun to jump into the dust devil. Turned out, not so much: a wee tornado that engulfed me in sand and arena debris billowed through my shirt, stuck to my sweaty body, and rearranged my hair.

Bobbie and Walt lived just down Squaw Peak Road from our place. I had known them and loved them from a time before I remember. In that era, important nonrelatives were given the honorary title of aunt and uncle, and they were mine.

My parents were active members of the saddle club and kept my fathers' two quarter horse mares in our corrals. Mom made dresses for us and western shirts for my dad, complete with top stitching and mother of pearl snaps. They rode often, competing in gymkhana events and sometimes we rode with them on overnight camping adventures. My sister sat behind the saddle horn in front of my father, and I sat behind my mother with my fingers in her belt loops. It was glorious.

When I was five, we moved back to my parent's town of Glendale, California, and the mares, Stormy and Candy, were sent to live with my dad's sister further north.

I am a child of the desert and feel most at home with dust devils, thunderstorms, cacti, and soft dry breezes. Yes, I know about snakes, scorpions, and Gila monsters. I just still love the night air and coyote song while sheet lightning dances across the sky and the stars—all the stars.

Those stars were best viewed from the top of the stacked bales of hay in the middle of the stable yard. When I was a bit older, I would share my very first kiss, stolen, by my childhood friend, Stevie, at the top of that haystack. He would mark the occasion by giving me a small moon stone to be worn around my 13-year-old neck. Sigh.

My sister and I finally landed in Phoenix and were scooped up by Aunt Bobbie.

She was a striking woman, older, to my eyes, though probably only 40'ish.

She was tall and grand and elegant. Her lush hair was silver grey over ebony black and swept up in a French twist held with hair pins, I have watched with open-mouthed wonder while she performed the magic of that hair wrangling. Sunlight catching on the hammered silver bracelet she always wore on her left wrist.

She had high cheekbones, a regal nose, and sun-tanned skin. Her eyes were dark and twinkled with delight at seeing us. Her lips parted into a wide grin. She was down on one knee with arms outstretched and she just inhaled us to her. She was quiet and I could feel her love. I was home.

I was awakened by the subtle change in the light, just when the orange started to seep into the sky and doves began cooing. My eyes opened to see the desert just outside of my window, start to move with the breeze. We have been here for a few days and my Uncle Walt has arranged a horse for each of us for our stay.

I crept out of bed and tip toed out of the room I shared with my sister. But I wanted to ride in the desert at sunrise alone. (she told me decades later that she knew I was sneaking out and leaving her behind).

My horse is not the flashy blue-eyed paint I thought I fancied, but Dee Dee a large bay quarter horse mare I had known forever. She was the correct horse for ten-year-old me. She was quiet and smart and had a great rump to lie back on when the trail allowed. She was magnificent.

The trail I want to ride headed east toward Squaw Peak Mountain. The sun was just rising, and all of the jackrabbits were standing at attention by the ocotillo and cholla cacti. Their ears are illuminated and back lit by the sun and they are tall on their hind legs, casting the most spectacular shadows. The trail was wide before the foothills and was used as a dumping ground for manure, so an easy amble without rocks or dust. I was quiet and so very contented. We walked along that trail for a long while. DeeDee shifted her head and shoulders toward home and I just smiled and giggled as we meandered that way. Of course, I dug my hands deeper into her mane. The smell of a horse and the morning desert remain with me to this day.

Aunt Bobbie was the best cook. I could smell breakfast from the tack room. When I stepped into her kitchen, she was frying bacon and eggs while heating the griddle for pancakes on a wood burning stove.

Coffee percolated in the pot with the glass nob on top for the adults, and there was a big glass of cold milk for each of us girls. After breakfast, we climbed aboard the hay wagon. Uncle Walt used a tractor to pull the hay wagon down the alleyway between the corrals and we girls tossed the flakes of hay to the horses.

It is a good day

Uncle Walt was a bit mercurial and had some good days, while other days we just left him on his own, tip toeing about.

He had a lovely palomino stud colt who liked to toss tires and lumber around the arena when he was let out to play. Uncle Walt tacked him up with a few gruff utterances then mounted and rode him for a bit. They were so smooth and graceful and quiet, both horse and man, to my ten-year-old eyes.

I turned 10 that summer.

Aunt Bobbie made my favorite angel food cake and whipped

the egg whites with a fork. She layered sugared, fresh peaches over the top.

Anyway, Uncle Walt had a pet cricket. We came into the house after dark and had sugared tea over ice in a metal cup, the chilled sides of the cup dripping with condensation, sugar resting at the bottom ready to run into my waiting mouth at the end.

We watched Ironsides, or Bonanza or The Rifleman.

We girls sat in front of the TV on the floor where the swamp cooler blew. Aunt Bobbie was in her chair stitching a shirt, and Uncle Walt sat in his chair sipping cold tea. Then we heard the chirping, every night at about the same time, until one night when we found the poor thing under the rag rug.

Uncle Walt only allowed women to board their horses at his place saying, "Boys are just trouble."

Most of the women were twentyish and all wore identical clothing. White button blouses with Peter Pan collars tucked into jeans with white lace up Keds.

But the best part was the tooled leather belts with a dainty silver buckles. No wait, the really cool bit was the tooling done at the very back of the belt with the letters of the girls' names spelled out. The young woman that I most admired had NAN in the small of her back.

The girls, after their ride, all gathered around the Coke machine outside of the tack room and drink Royal Crown cola. The machine had Nehi orange and grape and better yet Coke in small green-glassed bottles. I pull a Royal Crown.

Nan asked me to ride the desert with her at sunset. I practically vibrated with my good fortune at being chosen.

She was kind and sweet, and I felt included as we two rode out.

We took a trail north that I did not know. We wound around arroyos and up hills to a spot to watch the sunset. And we did.

As we turned back, we heard several angry rattlers warning us off the trail. Continuing away from the diamondbacks, we rode down the slope, slipping and sliding until we reached a small, dirt road and headed toward home.

It was Saturday evening, and we were passed by several Rowdy truckloads of beer-soaked cowboys.

They catcalled to Nan. She just smiled the most beautiful smile and veered off the road to a trail toward the ranch.

It was late and Aunt Bobbie left a plate of chicken fried steak, creamed pan gravy, mashed potatoes, and green beans on the stove for me. I felt so very grown up.

Early the next morning I crept into Aunt Bobbie's bedroom to gaze at one of the three photos hung on the wall. I have looked at this photo many times when no one was around. We are not allowed in the bedroom; adults were funny that way. I would not have another chance to study the mystery of this photo as we were leaving the next day.

The photo was of many girls about my age sitting in rows on the steps outside of a very grand stone building with carved pillars. They were all dressed in midi dresses and had dark braids tied up with ribbons. They did not smile or make faces, they sat stock still clasping their hands in laps.

Aunt Bobbie was standing behind me and put both hands on my shoulders. I jumped. She just smiled.

We sat at the foot of her bed and she told me the names of several of the girls and placed her finger on her face in the picture. She placed the photo back on the nail, took my hand in hers and gave it a squeeze. We walked to the kitchen in silence and made dinner together.

She never spoke to me about that time in her life. She never said what it was like to attend the school. She never spoke about the circumstances of leaving home. The photo spoke for her… all those little girls with solemn faces and beautiful eyes.

I would later understand more about what it was to be a Squaw.

I wear a hammered silver bracelet on my left wrist too.

UNDOMESTICATED

CYNTHIA FUNK

Become Undomesticated.
Unlock it my friend,
unlock it.
That box you are in.
Break free.
Gallop,
buck,
and express yourself.
Become Undomesticated.
Be wild and free.
Let your golden hair
flow in the wind and
run naked through the forest.
Feel the grass between your toes.
Come with me my friend,
feel the sun on your face.
Become Undomesticated.

(Inspired by Kathy Pike channeling the Horse Ancestors)

TAP TAP TAP

KIRSTEN ELIZABETH YEAGER

Death tapped me on the shoulder
As I drove home from work,
Snapping from my trance-like state
I startled with a jerk.
I turned to see who touched me
For I knew I was alone,
And faced an empty socket
Of an eye made out of bone.
Ivory teeth were grinning
An evil smile, you see,
Without a tongue, this specter said
"It's time to come with me."
I told him, "I'm not ready!"
My life lived only half,
His jawbone hinged wide open
In a criticizing laugh.
"This is not your choice, "He said,
"Your sands have just run out!"
Denying what he told me,
I shook my head in doubt.
"Traffic's jamming up ahead,
I know your brakes will fail!
You will fly straight through the glass,

On wreckage you'll impale!"
Right then the cars were stalled ahead
Panic and terror struck,
I found myself careening
Towards the tailgate of a truck!
I pumped my brake in fury
The pedal hit the floor!
His bony arms wrapped round me
When I tried to throw the door!
His insane laughter filled the cab,
As I braced for impact.
My eyes popped open, in my bed,
Alive! And all intact.
Shocked awake, and sitting up,
My throat still held a scream,
Death tapped me on the shoulder,
And gave me a bad dream.

THE MUSIC OF CONNECTION

NICOLE ARTZ

I am 10 years old, stomping down the stairs, stone-faced, ignoring my grandmother who sits on the chair in my parent's living room after receiving yet another round of chemotherapy for her stage IV colon cancer. Each day my mother has asked me to invite her down while I practice the piano after school and, each day, I refuse to acknowledge the request. I cannot tell them the reason- that I hold my grandmother in the highest esteem and cannot risk disappointing her.

My grandmother's life was music. She was the music teacher for the little Browning school in rural Missouri, the pianist for the one room church, the faultless player of Christmas carols at family sing-alongs every December. She was also the grandmother who played Parcheesi and Old Maid for endless hours, the one who always got the Old Maid card and gave it away with a soft amused chuckle, the one that I loved more than anyone. I pretend that if she does not join me in the basement, she cannot hear my imperfect renderings.

My grandmother also introduced me to horses, although they were never a passion of hers. When I spent time on her farm before she got sick, I could usually be found in the barn and paddock with the two farm horses and pony. I couldn't get enough of the smell, the sound, the feel of them. Just being near them was a joy. I didn't have much of an agenda other than to try and spend as much time with them as possible. Peeing and pooping in the barnyard was necessary in my "old enough to know better" point of view. Going up to the house was too risky- someone might suggest I do something other than hang out with the horses. Ignoring my grandmother's warnings, I occasionally climbed on when they got close enough to the fence that I could make a leap of it. When they ducked in the sheep section and walked under the low barn rafters, I did my best to pretend they weren't trying to scrape me off. After a few laps, I was reluctantly compelled to acknowledge that they were clearly not enjoying the ride as much as me.

A few years ago, when I was 45, my two horses stopped wanting to be with me. They started objecting to being tacked up for lessons. Initially subtle, signs of their discontentment escalated, until eventually they refused to come into the barn at all. I never cared about showing but I very much cared about improving my riding. I cared what others thought so I had stopped listening to my own conscience and instead followed the advice I was given: Ask—Tell—Demand. I stopped listening to my horse's signals that they weren't happy and began valuing perfection over connection in the unforgiving pursuit of "better". But what a price to pay, the loss of connection, my fear of judgment creating the chasm.

I realize now that my mother's suggestion to ask my grandmother to give me lessons on the piano was never meant to be about my playing - it was about connection. My grandmother just wanted to create memories with me. She didn't care if my staccato wasn't brisk enough or I couldn't play "The Entertainer" perfectly. She patiently waited upstairs every time, never saying a word, hearing every note just the same.

I was 13 when my beloved grandmother died. On our last visit to see her, I sat down at her piano with the beautiful needlepointed seat and the worn ivory keys. The same piano that she so cherished that, as a young mother in the midst of a house fire, she and my grandfather forfeited the rest of their belongings to save it. She was vacant now, a shell, glowing yellow with jaundice, confused, not eating, dependent on the caregiver for even her most basic needs. I wanted to give her a gift. I wanted her to see me in all my imperfection, to let her know how much I loved her. I played Canon in D with my fingers, my memory, and my heart. I played it for her. My grandmother's wrinkled face was transformed. No longer vacant, her expression was soft and radiant, full of joy, tears trickling down her cheeks. Music could still reach her. I could reach her.

I let go of my goals for my horses; remembering who I was before I forgot that just being with them was enough. I decided to place all of my focus on our relationship instead of the goal, even if it meant never riding again. I wanted, more than anything, to find the joy I used to know in their presence on my grandmother's farm. This was and is a decision equally full of vulnerability and hope. Accepting the vulnerability of being "not good enough" out in the open, for the hope of restoring and deepening connection with these beings that I treasure most feels awkward, embarrassing, exposed, but also non-negotiable.

I am stumbling my way along this new path, hitting many wrong notes, but my horses seem to appreciate this new me. Instead of "Ask-Tell-Demand" we are creating a different cadence, filled with notes both new and yet familiar to the little girl parts of me - presence, invitation, curiosity, patience, and choice. I am falling in love with each of my horses all over again, and when they choose to be with me, I recognize the precious gift they are offering. The music we are creating together now sounds more like a melody shared and traded between members of the orchestra, sometimes with unexpected improvisations. Their engagement, freely offered, fills me with the same kind of joy I saw lighting up my grandmother's face so many years ago. And I realize as I did at age 13, that it was never meant to be about perfection. The perfection is in the connection.

AN ENGLISHWOMAN'S VIEW OF AMERICA

SUE HILL

As an Englishwoman who has spent quite a lot of happy time in the U.S. over the past couple of years, I feel qualified to offer these observations about America which will hopefully entertain the residents of that fair land and also offer some advice for British travellers leaping across the pond:

Geography

Americans don't know the difference between England, Wales, Scotland, Ireland, Northern Ireland, Great Britain, the British Isles, and the United Kingdom. (A lot of British people don't know the difference either).

Language

There's no such thing as a "British" accent, which is mentioned in quite a few sit-coms (*Will & Grace, Friends* to name two). There is a multitude of very distinct accents across the country including of course the very basic Scottish, English, Welsh and Irish.

Many Americans think my very normal and perfectly proper English accent is Australian. As I am very fond of Australia, I don't react with too much disgust. (A well-timed "tut" does the job perfectly)

Weights & Measures

Something that the American people have is a sensible, (almost) uniform set of weights and measures. Miles, pints, pounds, and ounces. (Although I really don't understand "cups"). We have a hybrid of measures, courtesy of the EU. So we still drive in miles but we weigh in kilos and drink in litres. (But we can still buy a pint of beer). We measure our own height in feet and inches and weigh ourselves in stones and pounds and ounces. We find this all completely normal.

Travel

People in America generally don't go anywhere on foot. If you arrive somewhere without a car, you'll be cross-examined. When you explain that you've walked seven blocks to get to your destination, your host will look at you with shock and horror on their face and offer you a seat and some oxygen.

American trains are very long and not many of them carry people. If you're outside of a big city you might have to wait days between trains if they exist at all. In the UK you can generally get a train every twenty minutes from most reasonable sized conurbations. Although, perversely, most railway lines radiate out from London. So if you're 100 miles north of London and want to travel 20 miles west by train, you'll have to travel 100 miles into London, walk half a mile to the next major station and travel back 100 miles north on the next-door line.

I have had mixed reviews about public transport. In general, I've been told that long-distance public transport in America is not recommended for decent folk or those who wish to reach their destination in one piece. (It was an American who told me that)

Be careful when you use an American map – it might not be oriented North at the top and South at the bottom—I managed to walk a mile in the wrong direction once because the map was wrong. I'm proud to say that British maps are the best in the world. You wouldn't find a British map with north at the bottom and south at the top.

Car hire (rental) assistants have no concept of customer service, urgency, or the needs of jet-lagged and very tired customers. This observation might be the same for the UK, of course.

Any tiny town in America can proclaim itself a city with a sign at the roadside proudly declaring its name and the current occupancy. I've been told of a place called Lulu City in the Rocky Mountains that thrived for a single year in the Gold Rush and boasted a population of 200 at its peak of popularity. A city in the UK needs a lot more than 200 residents and must have a cathedral. (The rules have changed slightly in modern times)

American road number and speed limit signs are both in black letters on a white background. Pay attention when you're driving, or you could get into serious trouble. (Speed limit signs in the UK are neatly surrounded by a red circle for clarity)

Most American vehicles are huge. But this means that the parking spaces are usually huge too, which makes parking a compact hire car very easy. Hire cars are called rentals. Car parks are called parking lots. Boots (car boots) are called trunks.

In America, the driver sits on the left-hand side of the car. You'll need to drive in America for about 4 months before you stop making the mistake of getting into the passenger seat and wondering what's happened to the steering wheel. The same will happen to Americans driving in the UK. Americans have the disadvantage of having to negotiate tiny roads that were created by cows. (Yes, the first roads in Britain were created by animals' tracks!)

Some people in America carry guns, so don't get involved in any sort of road rage.

Motor bikers in America, unlike the UK, don't have to wear helmets. Don't call the police if you see a bare headed one. (See previous sentence)

Shopping & The Post & Tips

The money in America is all the same size and colour. Be careful. You'll think you're rich because you have a stack of notes (bills) in your purse (wallet), but if they're all "ones" you're actually skint. Conversely, if you pull out a bill for a tip, believing it to be $10 but it's actually $100, you might give the tippee a heart attack. Americans are usually enthralled by British bank notes—they are all different colours and mostly made of plastic. No, we didn't get them from Monopoly sets.

Everything in America is very big. Don't undertake a lengthy shopping trip in a mall (shopping centre) without the assistance of a walking frame if you're not 100 percent physically fit. Trolleys are called shopping carts.

I've never managed to buy an American postage stamp from anywhere except a Post Office. Post Offices are hard to find. Post boxes are blue and look like rubbish bins. Post is called mail in America. Except the Post Office which isn't called the Mail Office.

You must tip everyone for everything. Except Santa. I learned that from Judge Judy.

It's helpful to have a couple of smaller notes in your pocket when you arrive in America—if you're hiring a car, you might find that the driver of the shuttle bus will insist on putting your suitcases on and off the coach (even if he/she is smaller and older than you)—a tip is expected and appreciated. If you're American and visiting the UK, people other than taxi drivers and restaurant staff will not expect to be tipped. Check your restaurant bill before tipping—if the service charge is included, you won't need to leave anything else (unless you really want to)

You can't buy a pint of milk in a big supermarket in America. Be prepared to buy food and beverages in quantities of tons and gallons. (That's why American refrigerators are the size of a small car)

At the start of your trip, please be resigned to the fact that Americans cannot make proper tea. (Americans don't fully understand the concept of boiling water in relation to beverages—unless it's in your coffee). Their ignorance about tea shows because hotel rooms only have coffee machines and not kettles. Maybe there are many expatriates, because kettles can be obtained cheaply enough to make it worthwhile to purchase one for the duration of your trip. Oh—and take your own tea bags with you. For some reason most foreigners seem to think that "Lipton" is a trusted brand of tea. Just look in any supermarkets in Britain—can you find "Lipton" anywhere but the little section of fruit-flavoured teas? No. And fruit-flavoured tea is not tea. Bleagh. Just as coconut milk is not milk. Certainly not where a decent cup of tea is concerned.

The drive-through restaurants have enormous menus, the size of a map of the world, but they give you only three milliseconds to place your order. Mindful of the fact that the person behind you might be carrying a gun, you just ask for a bottle of water. The person taking the order will not understand your accent. Give up and drive to the window. They still won't understand, but it's a bit more entertaining to actually witness their confusion. Shout "I'm Australian" as you depart. Remember to drive on the wrong (right) side of the road.

There's a myth in the UK that the portions of food in American restaurants are huge. This is true. One restaurant meal in America would easily feed a family of four in the UK. Don't forget to ask for a doggy bag to take the leftovers home in. It'll sit in the small-car-sized fridge for a week before being thrown away, but at least it'll go into your trash can, not the restaurant's.

Toilets

Toilets are called "restrooms" or "bathrooms" or "powder rooms" not bogs or lavs or loos. You need to announce your intention to use these rooms rather delicately. For some reason, saying "I'm going for a slash" or "I need a pee" (or worse) is too graphic for the American ear. Ask "where's the restroom?" Don't worry, you won't need to take a rest there.

American powder rooms, for all the delicacy of their nomenclature, are surprisingly indiscreet. The doors have huge gaps underneath, and aren't very tall, and you can see through the gaps between the doors and the walls. It's very disconcerting to an unsuspecting foreigner.

Wildlife

If you're going to put up a sign saying, "Bears are more active at the present time," please have the decency to actually show us a bear. Just a baby one that won't hurt us. (The only bears you'll find in the UK are of the teddy variety)

Some of the spiders and snakes will kill you. Some of the wildlife will kill you. (The worst you'll get from UK wildlife is a bird doing a fly past and dropping a poop on your head. By the way—it's considered a lucky omen if it does happen, so smile)

American robins are big and have an orangey-coloured chest. British robins are proper robins with a red breast.

Weather

The weather can be crazy. Airports have tornado shelters in them. Whole towns are wiped out by tornadoes. People get lost and die in blizzards. The worse that can happen in the UK is a half inch smattering of snow that brings the M25 to a grinding halt.

In the Home (or Hotel)

The light switches are upside down. By the end of your three-week stay, you'll have just about mastered the fact that you push a switch up to turn a light on. When you get home, it'll take another three weeks to re-learn that you push a switch down to turn a light on.

The power sockets look like frightened ghosts with their two vertical slits for eyes and rounded "oh" mouths below. There's a strange dichotomy between the levels of trust placed in the general public regarding electricity. Obviously, Americans are not to be trusted with high power levels as their sockets deliver a measly 120V. In the UK we're trusted with a delivery of 240V. But in America you're trusted to have power sockets in the bathrooms (restrooms, powder rooms) and alongside sinks! This placement has been forbidden in the UK for quite some time—too many people were plugging appliances in and chucking them into the bath with any undesirable relatives/guests. If you want to do that in the UK now, you'll have to use an extension lead.

The reverse lack of trust is true with the sale of medicine. In the UK, we are not to be trusted with a pack size greater than eight adult doses of Paracetamol (Tylenol). If someone is hell-bent on committing suicide, they'll need to either stockpile their medicines over a number of days or take a long shopping trip visiting a number of different pharmacies. I suppose it's a good way of make sure that someone is really intent on doing the dastardly deed. I managed to find a huge tub of 200 Tylenol in the US when I had a headache. In fact, I couldn't find a smaller pack.

Taps are called faucets.

Oh—and very importantly—you won't find a ground floor in America. The ground floor is the first floor. Very confusing. There's no consistency, so you might find "L" on a lift (elevator) button for Lobby etc. It becomes a guessing game and a bit of a mystery tour. But I've yet to find a D for Dungeon.

Language

It's rumoured that George Bernard Shaw said, "The United States and Great Britain are two countries separated by a common language." He hit the nail on the head. The difference in spelling between Standard American English and Proper English is down to the foibles of one silly man (Mr. Webster). I think they should all just stop it now.

Bags are purses, purses are wallets and wallets are billfolds. Fanny packs are not used by gynaecologists. Don't worry if you hear someone ask, "where's my fanny pack?"—they haven't just had an unfortunate accident. Olive green trousers are described by Americans as khaki pants (pronounced "cacky pants"). If you have cacky pants in the UK, you have soiled yourself and you need to get to the bog and tidy yourself up sharpish!

Rubbish is called trash. Or garbage. Not sure of the difference between the two.

The People

American people are generally very warm and friendly, and once you've got past the "I'm not an Australian" stage, they are very welcoming.

There are quite a few Americans who don't know of Laura Ingalls Wilder. This is sacrilege. Her books should be required reading for everyone.

Men call old ladies "Ma'am". The only person who gets called "Ma'am" in the UK is the Queen. I quite like it, but it feels odd. I'm not the Queen.

America is great fun. I've had the best of times there. I haven't been killed by any wildlife or threatened with a gun. Yet. My favourite authors of all time are American. I have some wonderfully truly amazing friends across the States, and I can't wait to visit again.

Oh, and one final thing. Most Americans don't understand

sarcasm or irony. If your British witticism is met by a blank stare, be prepared to explain yourself, or just walk away. Try not to "tut."

LA NOTTE

LINDA DOUGHTY

I didn't want to disco dance.
Love songs left me cold
with their monosyllabic lyrics devoid of affection for
animals.
Vivaldi on the record player on a weekend morning,
that's what got me
out of bed.
Dream palomino, my Sawdust,
Dusty.
Moon reflective
silver halide
apparition.
I made promises:
To brush him until he gleamed,
To ride him every day,
To love him
constantly,
continually.
Real-life commitment
made in the dark of night.
I longed.
Interpretive dance
outside my bedroom window.

He ate grass.
He was content.
Just that. My conjured horse,
a figment of reality.
Jeweled Italian sunlight adorned la sonnambula.
My slumber blossomed gold.
Piccolo, mandolin,
violin.
Dusty blew apart
in brilliant fragments.
Sixteenth notes.
Backlit dynamics.
An exposition of glimmer.
Disco daylight in bell bottom pants.
Before I could dance
I was a seer.

MY WORDS

LASELL JARETZKI BARTLETT

I have had a mixed relationship with words since before I learned to speak them. What I heard and what meaning was understood by my little motor-sensory-attuned-otherwise-undeveloped communications byways were rife with contradictions. I was unable to understand or translate these ideas into sensible coherent expressions at that time.

A few years ago, I started creating and defining my own words. It was then that the light started to shine on an underlying urgency to have words match intention and meaning. I know they didn't match when I was little. What words were commonly used did not adequately help me make sense of my experiences.

How exhausting to spend one's life translating what people were saying from their English to My English. It certainly lay the foundation for my lifelong interest in helping people (and less verbal beings) navigate the murky waters between explicit and implicit memories. Our implicit memories live on in our bodies and show up—whether welcome or not—in our movements, facial expressions, intonations, emotional tones, belief systems, and more. Only when the implicit becomes explicit can we integrate and heal from the confusions and overwhelming experiences we nonetheless survived.

My earliest overwhelms were at birth and at six months old.

Both were near-death experiences. Both were definitively influential throughout my life: physiologically, socially, emotionally, cognitively, spiritually. Nowadays I'm playing on the edges of being done with looking to learn other people's maps. I want to travel unfolding into my own wild-born, self-mapping urges.

Below are many of My words with My definitions. I am still trying to make sense of the world. Having these as part of my "languaging" and meaning-making constructs brings a sense of ease deep in my belly. This feeling is different from feeling terrified that I'll get caught being Me.

I've put them in alphabetical order just because I can, and because sometimes creating order is comforting.

Beddy: Ready for bed.

Celf: The individual and unique experience of one's self at a cellular level.

Confirmotion: Livingness confirmed when in motion.

Deathimity: When all things are tinged by a flavor of awareness that death is close.

Disembounding: Becoming free from bounds, from emboundenment.

Emboundened: Wrapped tightly by unintegrated past experiences.

Frontiering: Stepping into the unknown and being with whatever is experienced regardless of pre-adventure fantasies and plans.

Fulling. Filling soul with friendly interactions rather than filling stomach with food.

Genhearting: Genuinely living and speaking from one's heart.

Heartnetting: When we experience connection through the placeless space of the internet.

Heartosity: Generosity of the heart.

Hecticity: The early stage of chaos, when one feels pressured to accomplish while unable to envision or enact the necessary sequence of events.

Infinitillion: How I count the vastness beyond a billion, trillion, kazillion.

Misattached: When maladaptive survival strategies have replaced actual relationship needs.

Pausating: The pulsing and repeated aspects of pausing.

Potenciating: Living one's power, manifesting one's potency.

Premoting: What we notice before a larger expression of emotion occurs. Prodromal state of emoting.

Prokinding: Lifestyle oriented to promoting kindness, offering ventral vagal co-regulating as often as humanly possible. Also called ProCo-ing and Ventralling.

Quirkumstance: Very unusual happening!

Remoting. Experiencing an emotion repeatedly due to stuckness in one's response system.

Spaceful: Expanded sense of openness and easefulness.

Spiralation: The elation that accompanies sensate awareness of spiraling directions of bones in motion.

Transtationing: The ongoing flow of changing states.

Treekulini: The spiritual experience of merging with the surging life force of a tree.

Ventralling: Being in the state of social engagement when the ventral vagal system is dominant. Also called ProCo-ing and Prokinding.

Wild-born self-mapping: Moving with abandon toward whatever elicits curiosity. Also called uncharted self-mapping and undomesticated mapping.

Wombmunity: The comfort of a safely containing womb experienced in community.

4 A.M.

KATE MCLAUGHLIN

It's 4 a.m. and I am sat on a rather uncomfortable sofa in a dimly lit room. It is meant to be "homely," but due to its location it can't help but be sterile. I am accompanied by my two good friends who are incensed by the causation of this trip, whilst also trying not to fall asleep. We have driven just over an hour to be here, winding our way through dark empty roads whilst trying to distract ourselves. I remember songs on the radio and reminiscing of shared times together prior to the last 28 hours. I am hunched over and numb. Numb from what has happened and disassociating myself from what is to come to be able to do it. My shoulders are stiff and all I can feel is a humming in my brain... this can't be real, maybe I imagined it, this doesn't happen to people like me... people like me... what does that even mean? Of course, it happens to people like me! Doesn't it? I'm not so sure. maybe it was just a misunderstanding... maybe, maybe, maybe. That is the funny thing when you experience a trauma, your brain tries to make sense of it, to compartmentalise it so that we can cope with it. At this point if I were a machine, someone would be instructing for me to be switched off then on again. It just feels I am in this void of nothing. I am a void of nothing.

A man enters the room, jolting me out of myself. He is very kind and reminds me of Ross Kemp. In any other situation we would be gossiping about this resemblance, but this is not the time. We listen in silence as he explains what is about to happen, and he then asks me questions about what has come to pass. I answer them dutifully and succinctly, ensuring no details are missed by my sleep-addled brain. I've answered a lot of questions today, posed to me by friends, by the police, by myself. How did I let this happen? That's a dangerous question to ask yourself. I didn't let anything happen. That implies consent, which from my recollection is a tad tricky to give when one is unconscious. The humiliation however started before consciousness was regained, and I am somewhat grateful that I haven't been able to remember all the details. Once I came to, well, that humiliation I was not spared from.

So how does a thirty-something divorcee end up in a situation like this? The world of online dating is both fascinating and terrifying. Being a savvy kind of person, and having negotiated some successful short term dates I felt confident that I knew what I was doing, so when I chatted to an eligible bachelor who wanted to take me for dinner somewhere I felt familiar and safe, I was in hindsight lured into a false sense of security. He was well dressed, well spoken, educated and good fun. We got on well and after dinner and a couple of glasses of wine in a restaurant I was a patron of, I started to relax and let my guard down a bit. He didn't look like a predator. did he? I left the table to use the powder room, and upon my return I had thought nothing of the fact that he had topped up my drink whilst I was gone—what a gentleman! He had been courteous and attentive all evening, bolstering my fragile divorcee ego, which I now come to understand was his grooming technique. The night becomes disjointed after that.

I woke up horizontal, face down and naked. I could hear a TV in the background and muffled voices. I tried to move and discovered I couldn't. As I tried to pull myself up onto all fours a wave of nausea overtook me and I vomited—projectile, clear vomit. Nothing like any hangover that I have ever had. I tried to get my bearings and was confused and relieved to find that I was at home. This relief was short lived as I sensed someone next to me in bed. I didn't remember coming home with anyone, in fact I didn't remember coming home at all. Before my jumbled thoughts had a chance to straighten out, he was on top of me again. He slid his arm around my waist, hauling me in the air and back against his groin. I've heard people say they don't have the strength to fight back, and I have never really believed them until now. A combination of whatever was in my system, and my instinct to survive meant that I physically couldn't defend myself. Surrender in this situation isn't consent, it is survival.

I vomited at least three times as he raped me again and again, finally dropping me back onto the bed and slapping my hind in mock praise. I had my head turned away from him the whole time, and I remember staring at my wall with silent tears rolling down my face thinking how the fuck do I get this person out of my house? He on the other hand, continued to watch television as I slid to the floor and crawled on my front to the bathroom. There, time was lost as I vomited continuously and with shaking legs managed to pull myself upright and put on a long t shirt. I defaulted into survival and "British politeness" mode as I offered him a drink and gently tried to coax him out of my house. I had almost succeeded as another wave of vomit took over and I ended up with my head in the downstairs toilet... in this moment he realised he had lost his wallet. His expression changed from one of smug superiority, to fear and then to anger. I managed to find it, thrust it into his hand and shoved him out of the door, which once closed I slid against and vomited on my floor. I managed to get back into my room, located my phone (which had a lot of missed calls and texts) and lay there trying to process what had happened. My children were with their father at this time, and my friend and I had a dating pact whereby we checked in with each other the next day. It was now early afternoon and having not heard from me, she came to my home and found me. Her expression said it all—I looked half dead, and her face crumbled.

When you utter the words, "I have been raped", it just feels bizarre—unreal and shocking. My friend encouraged me to call the police, I was hesitant to do so because what, in reality, could they do? As I now sat in this cold room talking to a detective, part of me wished I had just had a hot bath and pretended it never happened. However, I did report it, which is why my bedding, clothes, underwear, and dignity were being hauled off by the crime lab for analysis. My home had had numerous officers traipse through it, trying to be understanding but also doing their job. I just wanted to climb out of myself and for it to be over...it suddenly dawned on me in that little room that this was just the beginning.

From what I had told the Ross Kemp lookalike, it sounded like my perpetrator had done this before, as his technique was a little too polished. More tea was offered as we waited for the clinical team to collect evidence from me. If the humiliation of this ordeal wasn't enough, the necessary evil performed by two very sympathetic and professional ladies was the icing on the cake. Stripped naked, with every nook and cranny of my body documented and photographed, along with a physical examination is just soul destroying. I felt the only part of me that was still completely my own was my mind, and I was sure as hell not letting anyone take that away from me. More flashes from the camera in areas I never thought I'd have photographed, then I was given a complimentary goody bag full of wash things and toiletries to make me feel 'me' again and pointed to the shower room. I understand the sentiment and kindness behind these toiletry gifts, but it almost felt like a "sorry you have been raped, please do have a gift bag." It was going to take more than coconut shampoo to do the trick.

I then spoke to two detectives and went over what had happened again. They were kind and professional, and reassuring. They explained I would have to give them my phone, have a video interview at a later date, and asked a few other things, including how much did you have to drink, and what were you wearing? The answers were "not much to drink and a pant suit". I am wholly offended by this question. Do they ask nuns who are raped the same thing? I believed in the process, so I co-operated fully of course. I was then advised rape crisis would be informed and I would also have to attend the sexual health clinic for a myriad of blood tests and swabs, which would have to be repeated three times. I nodded, hearing the words but not really listening. I was back in my head, disassociating from everything that had happened, desperately wanting to go home, but equally desperate not to. My home was now a landscape I no longer recognised. I didn't feel safe, nurtured, loved and happy there. I felt vulnerable, embarrassed, sick, scared and worst of all guilty.

Every time I was asked about what happened, the onus was put upon what had I done to invite this attack into my life. What did I expect, I was serial dating, right? What were you wearing? You must remember something?

I didn't feel in control, I felt like a victim, and that isn't who I am. They arrested him and I had to give the formal video interview. I recalled every detail that I could as clearly and precisely as possible. The police said it was possibly the best video interview they had ever conducted. The Crown Prosecution Service however didn't agree. They thought I was cold and unemotional and therefore the chances of securing a conviction were small, so they didn't charge him. They also never tested my blood and urine to see if my drink was spiked. What they did offer was a restraining order so he couldn't come to my home. I felt let down and betrayed by the system that was supposed to protect me. Humiliated that this had happened to me, and angry... really angry. So, I took back control. I moved houses, stopped dating for a while and focused on myself. I do still have trust issues around men, and I feel lucky that I did not die. The police mused that I had possibly had quite a severe reaction to whatever he gave me, and he probably stayed to make sure I was not dead.

Am I glad I reported it? Yes and no. The whole experience is horrendous, but if it means his DNA is on file and it stops him doing it again—I can live with that.

I believe that date rape happens to more professional women aged 35-50 than we know. I understand the embarrassment, the self-shame, the 'I deserved it for being stupid' thoughts. I'm not suggesting that we force women to report sexual assault crimes, but I do think we need to realise the level of vulnerability it takes to do so. There is a fine line between establishing the facts and perpetuating a victim's negative thinking towards themselves. We need to support each other as women, and realise that the only person responsible for rape is the rapist—not the victim.

OCTOBER 22ND

ALYSSA REVELS

My womb was vacated twice
Once by the tenant,
Once with surgical precision.
Two heartbeats:
One still, one thriving;
One boy, one girl.
My thorn and rose in the pursuit of motherhood.
What a difference a year makes
For the same day is now refreshed.
From autumnal loss and grief
To harvesting the fruit of my labors.
A blessed birthday
A life, a love, a date renewed.
Goodbye, little one.
Welcome, little one.

WHAT HAPPENS
AFTER IT HAPPENS

CRISSI MCDONALD

"Rites of passage" is an expression we don't hear much anymore. There are rituals that have been lost the farther we trek into the industrial/technological age. Those occasions that, as I grow older, get farther apart and measure not how much life we have to live, but how much living we better squeeze out of life. The rituals particular to humans these days are celebrating achievements and witnessing deaths. These moments are easy to spot and feel and remember. How I relentlessly strived, how disciplined and focused I was, how we couldn't wait for the day to arrive. For me to arrive; a grown-up version of Christmas. A graduation, a driver's license, a marriage. A trip on my own to Europe, testing out the waters of adulthood.

I've learned what happens when something grows in myself. I've felt what happens when something throws me across its cosmic shoulders and takes me on a hike somewhere unknown and wild. Like a pregnancy has gone wrong. Years pass and another pregnancy is about to get derailed when I knew I'm no longer married to a man who I trust to be a father because he can't show up as a husband anymore.

Or the moment the veils lift in a great flash of light, and all my preconceptions of someone I thought I knew well are so beautiful, whole, and so lovely they make me ache.

The moment I've felt an animal, once defensive and fearful, lay its head in my lap or close its eyes as I stand with them.

The moment, when I once felt fearful and defensive, and then lie down in another's presence and welcome them with a heart to match their open arms. Or lie down in my own presence, feeling safe in my skin.

The moment one love dies, and another is born.

What happens is that I grew closer to our shared humanity. I now relish my shape and my breath. I weep from joy, or sorrow, but the despair has moved out through the small noises I can't stop from escaping when I cry.

Though at the time I called these moments of growth torture, they caused me to set up a metaphorical garage sale. All the things someone else told me I needed, I got rid of. All the beliefs I had adopted from elsewhere, from some other life, were discarded. At the end of many days, I stood looking at a stripped bare room. Holes in the walls where pictures (not mine) used to hang. The smooth whiskey voice of self-loathing and every other voice that sought to put me in my place weren't mine either, and so began the process of teaching my internal voice to use kinder words.

There's a point at which getting rid of clutter can also be an escape. I crossed that line many times. Whatever is at operation in this numinous universe, whatever Great Mystery has a hand in this great big beautiful messy life, it is the same hand that has guided me to know who I am. I don't have any other explanation because I have at times been weak. Cowardly. Passive, lazy, self-sabotaging. And while I have also been the flip side of all those things, I can't say with any certainty that I was the only force. There have been too many life preservers thrown my way for me to take credit for them all. I believe mystics used to call this Grace. It's probably still called Grace; such words give me pause, but as a recovering Catholic, I'm making my peace with them.

I've come to realize that many things happen after life's happenings. It's not the pinnacle. It's not the end. It's not a way station that we mistake for a home. What it is, what it blossoms into, is the knowledge of the beauty of who we each are and how we share this universe with a great mystery that can sustain us. While dearly held beliefs say more about us than about the beliefs themselves, I am also at the point in my gray-haired life that I am willing to admit that I don't know. The Great Mystery is now a comfort, and though my rooms aren't grandly furnished, everything in them is mine.

DEAR WOMAN

KRISTINA MARGARET

Dear Woman:

I understand you have been told again that you are too much, that your opinions have gotten you in trouble and you've been put in your place. I understand that you have been speaking out of turn, with wild ideas about who you think you are, and that you have the freedom to speak from the heart.

Well, woman, this you must know: every man who told you that his heart must be hard, will take you and rip to you shreds when you speak even a sentence of something they wish they could have said.

But; soft you see, has been treated with sin, and if you're speaking from deep down within, they will deflect all the pain, they hid through their lives with words and with weapons that will eat you alive.

Woman, you see how your true, honest heart will take what they can't say and rip them apart.

Deep in their eyes, they hide all their pain, projecting and blaming you with hurt and with shame.

But today, I am writing not to tell you all this, I am writing to tell, you must never quit.

You see, a heart with great sadness that remains soft, is a heart that can take madness and stop it from feeling lost.

Woman, a heart that becomes broken, and then becomes

strong, with the softness of loving when all has gone wrong, is a heart that can mend through the hurt and pain.

You see, there are some who stayed broken: who grew cold with control, belittled you as part of their game, kept you stuck in their hurt, their guilt, and their shame.

Please do not fear them, as they may never stop.

You must not blame yourself for the lies you were told, you're beautiful, powerful and your heart is pure gold.

Please, I beg you, keep standing back up, keep fighting for everything that lives in your gut. As the beauty within you is deep down inside, loving every part of you that is very much alive.

When defeated and tired, remember what's true, that your heart is the leader and it has love for you too.

The last thing I will say, that you should never forget, is to hold yourself tall; and, sweet woman, remember, you're stronger, braver and wiser, with the softness and all.

AND SO IT BEGAN

LAUREN WOODBRIDGE

She took a long breath and let it out with a whispered mantra. "I can do this, I am good enough, failure is a lesson." Her pen hovered over paper, her thoughts poised. A story from her past settled to the fore, Yes, she thought with a nod, this is the one and so it began.

My family has always been the eclectic and wild kind. If we had ever had a dollar to our name, we could even have been called eccentric.

I hold the much debatable honour of having lived in twenty-five different homes by the time I was twenty-five years old and that with only counting times we lived on the road as one home. I secretly loved it.

I had attended nine different schools by the time I was fourteen, which suited me perfectly as it gave just enough time to become properly reviled and ostracized before leaving to try again somewhere new. Did I mention I'm on the spectrum? I didn't understand it at the time, back then it was barely recognised, but it felt like the other kids could sniff it out on me. Like some cloud wafting before me that repelled kindness and left a giant "fight me" sign on my back. The nice kids soon learned that to like me was to join me in isolation and with how often I moved, most decided I wasn't worth the effort. I was in a dark place when this story began. I was angry, defensive, scared, and confused.

My only solace came from animals, I had my gorgeous young mare, Pearl, my pony of perfection; her coat always a glossy raven's black offset by her four white socks and clean white blaze. She was my best friend and confidante. I would come home from war and bury my face in her neck to cry. In my down time I would lie on her back and lose myself in the world of fiction. Turning pages to the lazy rhythm of her tail swishing away the flies. She would always whinny when she saw me; her ears would prick, and her eyes would brighten.

I was ten years old when I met her; she was just two and a half. I still remember the day like it was yesterday. My mum read the advertisement out to us describing two ponies, a brother and a sister. They were young, untrained, and most importantly, cheap. The moment mum described Pearl, I shouted my glee certain she would be mine.

When we went to the property, it was snowing, a rare event indeed for the season. The lady walked us down to the herd and showed us Pearl's brother Sonic first. They talked while my eyes raked the herd, hunting for my girl. I saw her and made a beeline away from my family to fall against her neck. My arms wrapped around her and I buried my face in her mane. I lost myself in a place I would quickly begin to call home.

I trained Pearl myself alongside my brother training his best mate and trouble incarnate, Sonic. We went to pony club and had a ball soaking up any knowledge we could, showing up anyone who stood in our way. I still had no friends, but when I was with Pearl, I didn't need them. Then we had to move again.

It was okay, I got to keep Pearl though we lived in the city now, but without the farm. Lazy afternoons just breathing together were replaced by adventures. We were intrepid explorers discovering every back trail and suburban shortcut we could find. Always testing the limit of how far we could get from our agistment paddock before the sun would set. We were always proving there was nowhere our brave ponies couldn't take us.

I was 13 when the fires hit. We raced to the paddocks as soon as we saw the smoke on the horizon. By the time we got there It was so dense I couldn't see my mum in front of me. She made us wait in the car while she disappeared into the inferno. We waited anxiously as the winds grew wild and the skies became as dark as night with only the red glow of the fires racing towards us to light the surrounding hellscape. Finally, her silhouette reached us. We leapt from the car to grab our ponies. "Saddles on and ride for home, NOW!" Mum shouted against the approaching roar of the flames. We obeyed without question.

The smoke cloyed our senses as we raced along the trails. We could barely see our path, but our ponies were as sure footed as ever. We raced past the police roadblock where our father was fighting to be allowed to bring the float through to us. Our bodies bent low across our ponies' necks as their legs stretched, outpacing the oncoming firestorm. We slowed only when we reached the suburbs and could no longer risk the pace. At last we reached our little suburban home. We spent the next week ready to evacuate at any moment. Our game plan was to ride the ponies to parliament house and park on their lawns. The only certainty in our minds was that we would never leave our ponies and they would never let parliament house burn.

It was nearing my 14th birthday just a few short months after the intensity of the bushfires. Our city had returned to seeming normality, when I was sitting with my father in the lounge room. We were watching a cop movie with a gorgeous German Shepherd as thecostar. I kept my eyes on the screen as I slid the conversation towards a tightly held wish. "That sure is a gorgeous dog."

"Yup."

"I wish I could get a dog like that."

"Sure."

My heart stopped.

"Could I get a dog like that?"

"Sure."

My mind raced but I kept my voice carefully calm, my eyes never wavering from the screen.

"Could I get a border collie?"

"Sure."

I let out the breath I hadn't known I was holding and just like that it was decided.

The hunt began for my dream hound, my constant companion and someone to watch my back when I couldn't be with Pearl. We passed on a couple of pups before we came to a small suburban home with three still available. I instantly loved the look of one of the girls, but my dad was right; she had chosen her home and had no interest in us. The other was a long-haired boy, no boys or long hair on my list quickly dismissed him. The last was a medium haired girl. Her bold white markings and calm, intelligent eyes made for a perfect match with my dear Pearl. I picked her up and looked at my dad. He nodded in approval and the decision was made. I cradled her in my lap on the way home and settled on the name, Gemma.

I set the rules hard and fast. With five siblings and a low-income household, there would be no sharing of Gemma, no confusion or mistakes made. No one was to touch or talk to her for the first two weeks. It seems strange but Gemma quickly learned to turn to me for guidance. In that time, we began creating an unshakable bond. She was mine and I was hers.

It was about then my mum went on a ride with a friend. "What's that?" she pointed to a sign hung on a post. A small yellow and red triangle. Tiny and previously unseen. "Oh that's the BNT." Her friend answered so casually never realizing her next words would turn our lives upside down.

The Bicentennial National Trail was a trail set just the year before I was born. It stretched 5330 kilometers from Healesville in Victoria to Cooktown in Queensland.

Mum came home and with a wicked grin announced, "We're going for a ride to visit Uncle Bill." The confusion was palpable. "Bill lives in Queensland mum."

"Yup 1600 kilometers, should take us about six months. Who's keen?"

And with that the daily torture that had been school ended. My brother convinced his school he had died, and I simply walked away. We all said we would try enrolling in distance education. We all knew it wouldn't work.

We began gathering the players. First came Gus, a grey Connemara, a carriage pony reject and too strong for kids. He was a soldier: a general born to the wrong era. He was known for grabbing the bit the moment he disagreed. His pride was palpable; his strength would hold our herd together. We would soon learn to have faith in his instincts and rely on his leadership.

Next was Curious, never a less curious horse had I ever met. His owner sent him with us through fear another spring would see him founder and die. We knew it was really because his uncontrollable nerves made him dangerous. You could feel his heart race at the slightest shift in shadows and to this day I admire him for the bravery he taught me.

Then we met Aly and Jubilee two gifts from a well-wishing friend. Two ponies with no future in sight.

Aly was a beautiful palomino mare, full of drama and fear. A princess with a dark and tormented past, she trusted no one. The first time they put shoes on her feet, they tied her to a tree, all four legs, body and neck constricted by ropes. She fought for her life, her eyes white rimmed with fear. I ran, too much the coward to stop them. I vowed I would never run again, and I would teach her to trust. By the time her next shoes were due, my twelve-year-old brother was able to do the job with the rope dangling and her eyes soft, holding her foot lightly for him. She gave me the gift of trust, a powerful thing hard won and easily lost.

Jubilee was a funny creature: small at twelve hands and the oldest of our little herd. He was in his early twenties and his owners sure he wouldn't make the winter. He proved his worth many times over and the trail brought him to life. He would jig jog for hours on end, with no sign of fatigue. He would always push to keep going. It was a challenge to stop him from pulling his rider forward out of the saddle when he was on the lead. It took him months to learn to walk. He taught me about heart and never discounting those who appear less than they are.

There was of course my perfect miss Pearl: our trustworthy staple, my best friend, my aunty, and my mother. She was ever reliable, taking the lead through any obstacle that would make the others baulk. Nothing phased her: not cyclones, floods, snakes, or man-made monstrosities. She was our rock and showed me that we can't always control those we rely on, sometimes we need to let go and have faith.

Pearl's brother and my brother's best mate, Sonic, was our prankster and class clown. He would tease the other ponies mercilessly until Gus would give him the look. He was always pushing boundaries and stirring the pot, but he was as loyal as they come. He would do anything for my brother and always had Pearl's back. Together they made our little pack of reject ponies into a family.

Not one month after my fourteenth birthday we were ready to leave. Gemma, still a tiny pup, sat atop Aly's back nestled amongst the packs: a rather hodgepodge of back packs strapped to a saddle.

I sat beside her on Pearl, of course. A huge grin plastered on my face. Ready for anything, sure this would be better than school at least.

My mum rode Gus, her short, soft stature made tall and proud on his back. Her hand confidently held Curious as he quivered like a leaf.

My brother rode Sonic as he and Jubilee danced and jostled. His little Chihuahua, Chicka, was prancing among their feet, ready to run the whole way with a bounce in her step.

Ready to write the ride, I lay my pen down with an exhaled breath, noting the lines on my older hands. The sun warms my back as I look out to the paddocks at the ponies grazing contentedly. Pearl's raven-black coat, though aged, still stands out starkly against the bright green grass. As the adventure begins again, on the page, this story must end, for now. I must go and visit an old friend.

A LONG TIME SINCE

PATTI BREHLER

we stand hugged by steam while warm water streams
she brushes my belly with gnarled fingers
your skin, she says, look at it
i look down, a few pounds pouchier than a year ago
it's so smooth
i glance up, her hand swipes lightly across her breasts
not like my ugly skin
i consider her life-pocked body, and think, i came from her and
left
cells of my own behind
lived in, mom, not ugly

she bends, hangs on to the shower chair as I scrub her back,
her neck, her bottom, her legs
a long quiet moan wells, like a breath of breaking ice
across a frozen lake

she turns to sit, and groans,
an ancient oak in protest of the winter wind
she rests
she scrubs the rest of her body herself

when she can, she stands
one hand grasping a grab bar, the other clasping mine,
a slow dance, swapping places

she faces me, eyes closed, wondrous
warm water wetting her hair, gray streaks melting into white,
my fingertips massage shampoo into her blemished scalp,

a sigh
slips
in delight,
her child-like smile washes me
with light

DAUGHTER TO MOTHER

MARY MCGINNIS

Feminists, I said, I was nobody's baby.
I had a body, but I was not just my body.
Nobody's string dragged through my dreams.
If it had, it would have been a length of red licorice
which I adore.

I had debated between sun and water,
and sun won out.
No tattoo, though someone could have talked me into it.
I was a plump baby once,
worried for years I was too plump.

What am I skirting around?
Ghosts, emptiness, bloody steak?
Fajitas?
Right near my left eye is a pen mark
from a fifth grader when I leaned too far to the left.

Did we exchange blood?
Probably not. Never did big drugs.

It was hard for my mother to be a mother:
she wanted me like we want rain in New Mexico,
enough for the garden, not a flood,
not too much -
she didn't like mud.

She did like plays, a well-set table,
square rolls,
tiny salt and pepper shakers at each place setting,
good, tall candles.
It was hard for her being a mother.
We've said goodbye so many times.

AUTHENTIC VOICE

Speak the truth, even if your voice shakes.

Maggie Kuhn

KINTSUKUROI

LORI ARAKI

She came quite suddenly into the world after resisting whole heartedly for a considerable time. Once she remembered that she had agreed to this, the journey was quick though not entirely painless. Falling into waiting hands, the sudden stop, the brightness, the cold, the shock of separation stunned her into quiescence, and she immediately began to forget.

Hands that encompassed the entirety of her dried her pelt and took her measure, not realizing the inadequacy of their measuring tools. Passed back to her mother, she felt slightly less alone. After some time, her pelt was noticed and remarked upon.

"Lanugo," the doctor explained, "it will shed on its own."

She couldn't recall agreeing to losing her pelt and was quite certain she didn't want to. What would keep her warm? Who was she without it? Swaddled in soft blankets, hiding her even softer coat, her mother whispered, "Hello, Eloise. I'm so glad you're here."

She felt the most powerful of mortal magic wash over her, flooding her tiny body so full that she imagined her heart might burst. Instead, to her surprise, it expanded. And just like that she was anchored to the world.

Her days and nights blended together, everything new and often overwhelming. She met her father, her sisters and brothers, her grandparents and was completely baffled. She had trouble separating them from each other, seeing them at once both inextricably connected to her and each other, yet each apart, distinct, separate. The separation was painful, and she reached out to draw them all in.

She took root in her family and grew depth and height and weight.

The neighborhood dogs came to her when she called. She would gather them together, teach them tricks, pretend they were performers at the circus. For a while she imagined them lions and she a fearless lion tamer. But she looked in their soft, brown eyes and saw sadness. "Are we not enough as we are?" She gave up the idea of 'lion tamer' and was happily, a dog tamer. They were happy to pretend to be wild for her.

Her mother would call, and she would say goodbye to them, seeing eye to eye as they sat in a line before her. She would hug each one, thank them for participating in her games, and admonish them to be good dogs. She never said that she loved them. They knew.

When her grandmother was ill and in the hospital, her mother took her to visit. She was excited about riding in an elevator and seeing her grandmother again. The elevator doors closed, and the space rose sharply, startling her and knocking her elbow on the cold, hard wall.

She followed her mother to her grandmother's room and, undaunted, she climbed on the bed to give and get hugs. Her grandmother cried out and Eloise was heartbroken to have caused her storytelling grandmother pain.

Not long after, her grandmother came home to end her days with family. Eloise would visit, careful not to hug, and took over the storytelling. Until one bright, spring morning, her mother said, "Eloise, Grandma passed away last night."

She didn't know what that meant. But her trip in the elevator became conflated with illness and death. She learned to fear. Having lost someone she loved, she remembered what death was and grew fearful of both small and large things, elevators, her own heartbeat, her sisters, and loss.

As she grew, she aspired to be an athlete, an artist, a scholar. She read voraciously, practiced with pencil on paper and leapt from swings as they reached their apex. She practiced music and invisibility. She studied math and levitation. Neither went as well as the music and invisibility.

One summer, she became desperately ill. She lost track of time, becoming weak until her voice silenced completely. She was unable to walk without assistance. Time ceased to exist. She remembered a lounge chair in the yard, swaddled with blankets under the hot summer sun too weak to sit up yet every cell in her body vibrant with life.

A woman came to visit, standing before her, the sunlight forming a halo around her. She spoke gently but Eloise seemed to hear more with her heart than with her ears. "Listen to your heartbeat, Eloise. Listen and breathe with it." So, she did and once again felt the power of her own heart as she had when she was small.

She stepped back into the world and shed her invisibility.

Eloise listened and learned and grew. She moved through life in awe of the beauty around her, listening to the prompts from her heart, overflowing with gratitude.

She believed her childhood was unremarkable. She was shocked to learn that people didn't always mean what they said, that sometimes parents were heartbreakingly cruel to their own children, and those children sometimes grew into adults who couldn't comprehend kindness, could neither give nor receive it. Eloise became less and less of herself. Her wonder and joy in the world became weak, tenuous, the world shrouded until one day she was shattered.

She became invisible again.

It would take a decade to recover from four small words. "I. Don't. Love. You."

She took her hard-earned invisibility and left.

Eloise didn't know how but she paid her bills, connected with friends, and even made new ones. She took care of animals, quite certain that if it weren't for them, she would have shrunk to nothing and disappeared forever. She began the painful work of piecing her heart back together.

She developed the habit of leaning her forehead on the soft, warm coats of horses, just trying to move air in and out of her lungs. The horses began looking back at her to help her breathe. Sometimes she would lift her head and see colors again.

Her dog died. She remembered the words, "I don't want to be around when your dog dies." The fragile glue holding pieces of her heart together gave under the pressure.

She got a new dog, so alike and so different from her old one. She held him to the standard of the old dog and knew it was unfair. His heart was so large he accepted it and loved her completely. Was she ungrateful?

Her mother died and her siblings joined together to strengthen each other and support her father. Every time her father spoke of her mother he would cry. She would rub his shoulders and let him. One of her sisters passed. Her father followed not long after. Her cat died. The Years of Loss and Devastation. Was she ungrateful?

Life no longer flowed toward her. She would study and cry, pray and rail. Filled with anger and grief she would beg for help. She would rebuild her broken heart only to feel it disintegrate in her hands.

Her neighbors asked her to take care of their dog. She remembered her circus dogs and wondered what it would be like to feel the connection she had had as a child. She went through the motions of feeding and watering. She trimmed the dog's claws. The owners returned, thanked her. Was she ungrateful?

She awoke with a start, dreaming again. But no, not a dream. Someone was knocking. Three a.m. She opened the door and her neighbor's dog came in. She laughed. She couldn't remember the last time she had laughed. Then she cried. The dog returned three more times.

Strays showed up, a hound dog, a raccoon, some more dogs, three horses, a snake, a few people, hummingbirds. She began to run again but couldn't bear to draw. Music had stayed with her always. She was grateful.

Then, one day, it happened. A toddler, on her own two feet veered towards her, smiling, stopped before Eloise and raised her arms to be held. Her father scooped her up. Eloise smiled and said hello. The mother looked Eloise in the eye. And just like that, she could be seen.

Eloise continued to glue pieces back into her heart. She would create new pieces to fill in the gaps, cobbled together from helping someone, from seeing a sunset and recognizing the vibrancy of colors, from horses galloping through their fields. She imagined these new pieces like stained glass, sealed in place with silver instead of lead, bringing light into her broken heart and hoped that soon she would hear it's beat again, and the glue would be strong enough to hold.

"You are cordially invited to the wedding of…"

She closed her eyes, listening. She thought about returning to the place where her destruction began and felt her heart vibrate. She prayed that her heart would hold and walked very carefully all day, cried herself to sleep, and awoke feeling fragile.

The phone rang, a rare occurrence. "Eloise, please come to my wedding. I miss you and it would mean so much to me if you would come."

She felt the words leave her lips like she was speaking a language she didn't know, her brain backpedaling—no, it will hurt—as fast as she said, "I wouldn't miss it." She closed her eyes and heard her heart thump. One time. Two times. Three times.

She packed her dog and her things and drove for two days. She visited people she had missed and the important places, all the while feeling out of place, a stranger. As difficult as it was, she enjoyed the wedding, loved the people there, and received more hugs than she had had since she had left.

She traveled to the wilderness where she had spent so much

peaceful time, breathing in the power of the mountain, the sea, the sky and breathing out gratitude. Was she still ungrateful?

She picked up an orange-brown rock nestled among the green serpentine, sun warmed, smooth and sharp in her hand, intending to carry it until it no longer felt different from herself. Instead she picked up a green one, red dirt stuck to one side, ultimately putting both in her pocket. The dog panted at her side, sometimes whining in anxiety or excitement, she was no longer certain which.

Seated on a rock, a creosote bush blocked part of her view of the valley stretching for miles below. The bush was beautiful in its way, its dried leafless branches piercing through the live ones, being both dead and alive at once. Creosote, the zombie of the plant world.

She waited in the sun, hoping for an opportunity to heal or at least to accept. The mountain side was still beautiful, still powerful. She worried that perhaps she had changed too much to ever feel the sort of peace she'd felt here so many painful years ago. The tears that had threatened on the drive up finally began to fall. She looked at her dog, hot and whining, wondering how long it would take for the mountain to do its work of healing and wondering if she could stay that long. Having forgotten tissues in the car, she wiped her eyes and nose on her sleeve.

"Can you take some of my burden, Mighty Mountain?" she asked. "It's heavy and I don't want to carry it anymore."

After a moment, she wondered at her words. "Can you," not "Will you."

"Are you capable of bearing my wounds?" But not, "Will you help me?" And "I don't want to carry it." Not, "I'm not capable of carrying it," or "It's crushing me with its weight."

A cool breeze blew up the mountain, hinting at the ocean that she knew stretched across the horizon beyond the next row of mountains. She thanked it, knowing that once she walked with her whole being full of grace and gratitude for the beauty that filled the world and also knowing it had never been enough for the people who populated it.

"Am I enough for you, Sacred Mountain?" she asked as the tears that had stopped began to fall again. Realizing at some point she had picked up another rock, she clutched it tightly, an anchor to her old, unbroken self.

RED

EVE ALLEN

I've moved to a new place in time for the holidays and I have two Christmas trees. The small LED-lighted tree sits on my kitchen bar, surrounded by a few of my decorations. In the center of the decorations is The Final Present. The Red One. The last gift my mother will ever give me.

My story starts more than a year ago.

When someone you love is living with a looming deadline to die, each holiday or birthday begs the same question: Is this the last one?

My mom was in her nineties, with dementia, taking every step of the present in borrowed time. Every Christmas, Thanksgiving, her birthday and my own that came and went, I thanked God for another one with my mom.

Despite her mostly absent hearing and dementia, my mother fussed that she should be allowed to drive. We didn't let her. Since she was no longer able to go out and shop for my presents like she used to, I started buying a few things for myself at Christmas, giving them to her to wrap, and we pretended they were from her to me.

Those last years, when we sat together on Christmas Eve night to open presents, only one of us was surprised by what was in each festively wrapped package we traded. I'd be lying if I said it didn't sting. No matter how many decades I had banked as an adult, I still wanted my parents to give me a present that made my eyes wide with delighted anticipation as I tore into it, not knowing what they had chosen just for me.

Last year, during one of her clearer moments when she realized Christmas was coming, she insisted she wanted to buy me some presents. I realized this was likely the final chance for her to shop and for me to enjoy the fruits of her labor. I handed her a wad of cash and asked the wonderful lady who helped me take care of her to take her out for a shopping trip. My mother asked what I wanted. I replied, "Whatever you think I'd like, Mom. Who knows me better than you?" When pressed for at least an idea, I suggested an ornament, and recommended they visit Hallmark and Pier One.

A few hours later, there were three presents wrapped and placed by the tiny artificial tree I bought at Walgreens. Christmas had become too different and often sad to bother with the giant artificial tree for years.

Christmas was delayed a few days because I was ill, but the night finally came where I called my mother into the living room for our gift exchange. Mom sat on the couch with a blank look on her face, while I explained that it was Christmas and handed her a present. While appreciative of the decorative box I filled with her favorite miniature Hershey's chocolates and kisses, she took a few and handed the box back to me. Despite my repeated assurances the box of candy was hers to keep, she couldn't quite grasp that it was a gift to her or why I was giving it. I didn't see the point of continuing and asked if she wanted to go back to bed. She did.

I managed to wait until she left the room before bursting into tears. Moments like that ripped a hole in my soul that I wasn't prepared for, even if I knew they were eventually going to arrive like a burglar at my bedroom window at two in the morning. I accepted that this Christmas was either going to be the last semi-coherent one for my mother or, possibly, the last one at all.

After a couple of very dark emotional days, I opened two of my presents and was delighted with what my mother had chosen for me. Even in her dementia, she still knew my taste. One package was a collection of three miniature boxes, each covered in a glossy wicker type material with a featured bright jewel tone. Pier One always could catch my eye with merchandise like that. To be honest, I cannot remember what the second present was, but I know I liked it.

The third present remained, encased in glittery red wrapping paper. I left it unopened, not entirely sure why. As the days passed and a new year began, I realized I was saving this present, saving Red, as I began to call it. Saving it for when my mother was gone and there would be no more shopping excursions for her or packages under the tree she had selected for me.

Red sat on the built-in shelves in the living room for weeks. Every day I would see the present. I didn't know if I would be overcome with a need to unwrap it immediately, or if I would just feel the time was right to unveil it on some unspecified day weeks or months later. Certain I would know when the time was right, I moved the present to my bedroom closet.

My mom died this past July.

I moved shortly before her death, after she had been safely ensconced in a nursing home, and the last several months since she passed away have been about grieving, crying, sorting through earthly possessions, and wondering just when in the hell does it get easier?

I decided to put up my Christmas tree this year. Part of me was quite excited. I love the pageantry of hanging the lights and garland, but my favorite part is going through the ornaments.

If you are at my house when I'm unpacking them, fix yourself a large drink and sit down, because I will tell you the story of every ornament I own. You'll learn which ones are childhood favorites, which ones were a gift from someone special, which ones were homemade and which ones I bought myself. If you are bored by this recitation, I won't notice because I'll be too busy grinning like a goofball as I pull out the next ornament and search for the right place for it on the tree.

My six-foot artificial tree looks amazing. To my surprise, I didn't cry when I decorated the tree. Instead, I got a little misty-eyed in anticipation of experiencing the daily joy of seeing a Christmas tree in my living room again.

I was correct that I would know when it was time to open that shiny red present. Tomorrow night, Christmas Eve, is the big night. I know it's an ornament, because mom slipped up and told me that, but I don't know what kind.

I know I'm going to cry. I may end up going into an ugly cry; the kind where I want to do it alone because no one should witness the howling that comes from the loss of someone I love so much.

I'm hopeful I will also experience joy. To be honest, I'm a little intimidated by what emotional process lies ahead. I may have to mentally strap myself in and ride it like a roller coaster. But I am ready. Strike that. I am as ready as I will ever be.

Come tomorrow night, I will sit down, pour a glass of the red wine my mother loved, and open the last present she will ever give me. I will open Red, and if the universe works the way I like to think it does, I know that my beautiful mother will be there witnessing my tears and joy.

THE SWING

KIRSTEN ELIZABETH YEAGER

Safe within
My cage of ribs
I kept with me
A tiny bird.
Singing bubbly,
Joyful songs
My silent heart
Had only heard.
Every day
She'd sit and sing
Upon a tiny golden swing
And fill my chest
With everything:
Hope and love
And wondrous things.
After about a month
Or two,
I showed my little bird
To you.
She jumped upon your
Loving hand
Still singing songs so sweet.
You without a single word

Took my happy little bird
And promised me you'd love her
You vowed your love complete.
Stealing from me my breasted friend
And disappearing without end,
I felt the loneliness within my chest
Began to ache.
As the winter turned to spring
She without her golden swing
Began to wither,
Lose her song.
Her tiny heart did break.
I loved and trusted you that day,
Even when you walked away,
And hoped you would return
Bringing back my feathered friend.
But hopes and dreams are like
The breeze
You floated off with such an ease
Never giving second thoughts
That this would be our end.
Carelessly you caged my bird
In selfish darkness without word
Alone afraid and longing
For the sunlight up above.
And I waited hours, it seems,
On promises and broken dreams
And all the beautiful
Wondrous things
You promised me of love.
And my tiny little bird,
In darkness wilted without word,
Tucked her head on heavy wing
Giving up her song.
But I alone did not forget

Your final words
Your lame regrets
Leaving the little bird of mine
To die within the dark.
But you see this little bird
In silent darkness
Without word
Escaped your cage
And took to winds
Like storms upon her wings
And fast into my bloodied chest
Never stopping flight to rest.
My tiny friend drew a breath
And sang a loud once more.
I, alone, sat up to gasp,
My soul returned to me at last,
Knowing that your hold on me
Had finally met its end.
And safe within my cage of ribs
My little bird can sing again
Joyful, wondrous, bubbly songs
And promises of love.

SORRY ABOUT THAT!

ANN LEVY

Transcript of the June 1, 2019 meeting of the Sorry About That Club, Argus, Ohio, 7:30 PM.

Present: President Arnold Heller, Vice-President Evelyn Milkus, Secretary Dan Foyt, Treasurer and Hospitality Chairman Susan Meyerson, various club members in audience

(sound of gavel)

MR. HELLER: This is the June meeting of the Sorry About That Club. Our club's mission is for our members to admit to and learn from their mistakes. We help members realize that mistakes are an essential part of life. The meeting will now come to order. All rise for the Pledge of Allegiance.

(whispers from behind the table)

MR. HELLER: Oh, okay. No problem. Ladies and gentlemen, no-one remembered to bring the flag, so tonight's ledge will be replaced with a moment of reflection. I guess the first apology of the night is ours! We're sorry!

(laughter, a call of "It's OK" from the auditorium)

MR. HELLER: All rise, as we now reflect on our good fortune to be living in this great country, and also on our understanding and appreciation of the rights and responsibilities that we have as citizens. We are all one family of humans, and so we need to treat others, as well as ourselves, with respect and love.

(silence, then all sit back down)

MR. HELLER: The goal of our group is to realize we all make mistakes, admit to them when they happen, apologize, fix what we can, and move on. Evelyn, who wants to give us their apology first?

MS. MILKUS: First, we'll hear from Sam Wilkey. Sam, the mic is yours.

MR. WILKEY: Good Evening, Members of the Board, Ladies and Gentlemen. I actually have several apologies tonight. I believe I know many of you. My name is Sam Wilkey, I am the weatherman for Channel 12, WOAH, here in Argus. I also write a weekly column about making and maintaining beautiful gardens in the Argus News. I work very hard to ensure I make accurate weather predictions, but I am right only about 50%. I'm sorry for that, and I always to strive to do the best I can. Last month I predicted a late-spring frost, followed by a thunderstorm. The next two days were the hottest in May that Argus has seen in the last 20 years. I am very sorry for my wrong prediction. I am also sorry that I covered all my plants and left them covered the next day until I got home from work. All my flowers in my garden died due to the heat that built up. The heat also killed the flowers in my hanging baskets, buds and all.

MR. HELLER: Oh, Sam, I'm sorry to hear that. I thought your gardens and your hanging baskets were destined to be especially gorgeous this year.

MS. MILKUS: Keep trying, Sam, we know you're doing your best. We Argusites appreciate the effort you put into your predictions. I'm sure no-one would want to see you stop.

(murmurs of agreement, smattering of applause from the first rows)

MR WILKEY: I got some good from this, though. A family of birds decided to build their nest in one of the empty baskets, so I've been leaving seeds out for them. And I'm thinking of adding a segment on birds and their relationship to healthy gardens in my next column. I'm researching how to attract them and how to help them. I want to help us make Argus more nature friendly.

MR. HELLER: That sounds great, Sam, you're making the best of a bad situation. Good luck in your new project. Well, time to move on. Evelyn, who apologizes next?

MS. MILKUS: Next is Les Petro, who owns the Argus Bake Shoppe.

MR. PETRO: Thank you, Evelyn, Members of the Board, Ladies and Gentlemen. I made a big mistake in my bakery, for which I am very, very sorry. I put salt instead of sugar into a birthday cake for an order for Sonia Goldbury. It was for her daughter Shayna's second birthday party.

I am so sorry! I would never hurt Shayna, she is just the cutest little thing I have ever seen, all her blonde hair, and those pigtails. Also, did you know she got a new puppy? He's adorable, all roly-poly. He just makes me laugh and laugh. Sonia and Shayna brought him in to show me that they forgave me for the cake disaster. His name is Jasper, and he pees inside sometimes still, so Sonia had to run outside with him a couple times while she was in the shop....

MS. MILKUS: Les, he does sound sweet. But back to your apology. It sounds like the Goldburys forgave you, and maybe you have learned something from this experience?

MR. PETRO: Yes, I have learned to keep my sugar jar way across the room from my salt jar! Maybe I could even put the sugar into a jar that looks different from the salt jar. Then I would never mix them up again.

MR HELLER: Those are great ideas, Les. And you showed us that everyone needs to admit accidents happen, that no one's perfect. Just say you're sorry about it, do what you can to fix it, and move on.

MR PETRO: I'm making an "I'm Sorry" cake, for free, for the Goldburys. And I'm trying a new recipe for dog biscuits, for Jasper.

(murmurs of agreement, a call of "You got this, Les" from the auditorium)

MR. HELLER: Thank you, Les. Evelyn, who's next?

MS. MILKUS: Our last apology tonight is from Rhonda Aynesforth, who owns Hair by Rhonda.

MS. AYNESFORTH: As you may know, I'm a new member. I joined last month when I opened my shop downtown. I'm on Second Street, near Main. I want to show my appreciation for your support, so any member of this group who patronizes my shop will get a 15% discount.

MS. MILKUS: Thank You, that is a very kind offer, but not necessary for you to join our club. Welcome to our group.

(murmurs of agreement, several calls of "Welcome!" from the auditorium)

MS. AYNESFORTH: Well, I offer it because I'm glad of the support I get from this group, and I'd be happy if I could help you in return. And I'm very glad that I joined this club. May I make my apology now?

MR. HELLER: Thank you again, and go right ahead, Ms. Aynesworth. We're all friends, here.

MS. AYNESFORTH: You all may know that opening a new shop can be exhausting. I admit, I was tired from the move to Argus. And I'm too nervous from all that's going on to sleep well. I'm not trying to make excuses, only being honest, setting the stage for my apology.

A few weeks ago, right after I opened my shop here, one of my first customers came in for a change to her hairstyle, but she didn't know what she wanted. She just knew she wanted something different. So, we went through some pictures on her phone, and found a great cut for her. I think it would have been very flattering, I really do! Well, we decided it would look even better with highlights, coral, was the name of the color. Well, the highlights went very badly. Her hair turned......

(Pause)

MR. HELLER: Go on, it's going to be okay. We're all here for you.

MS. AYNESFORTH: It turned orange. She looked like Ronald McDonald. I tried to fix the color, but she has very thin, fine hair and it was so damaged by the highlights that the fix made her hair fall out. She's bald now, because of me! I comped her visit of course, and, more importantly, I apologized. A bunch of times. I hope she knew I feel terrible about it. She decided to go home until her hair grew back. I haven't seen her since. I'm trying to move on, but I still want to cry every time I think of it. I just hope she comes back.

MS. MILKUS: Oh, I'm sure she will. These things happen. And you offered to fix it for her, I'm sure she's just waiting for her hair to grow back in.

(murmurs of agreement from the first two rows)

MS. MYERSON: To be honest, I know the woman you're talking about. I went to school with her. I saw her at the diner the other day, and she was wearing the most gorgeous hat. I told her I loved it, and she took me aside, whipped it off her head, and she was bald, as bald as my Nana Sara! Then she told me what had happened and how you tried to help her, and how you cried, and how she doesn't blame you. I don't think you have to worry at all. She's always had problems styling her hair, even in school it was always crazy and all over the place. She confessed to me that she kind of likes being bald, that she thinks it's such a neat feeling when she runs her hand over her head. But she's thinking she might not like being bald in the winter. So she's letting her hair grow back. She showed me the picture of the cut you both had picked before the color fiasco, and I loved it! She said she can't wait for her hair to grow back enough. She also said I should go to your shop.

MS. AYNESFORTH: What a relief. I'd hate to think I made an enemy of that nice lady. I'm looking forward to working with her again. And, by all means, please do come in!

(applause, a call of "Hey, I need a haircut! See you tomorrow." from the auditorium)

MS MYERSON: I'll call tomorrow for an appointment.

MS. AYNESFORTH: Oh, I have just the cut in mind for you, I'll show it to you when you come in.

MR HELLER: Can't wait to see your new hair style, Susan. Moving on, is there anyone else? No? I think we're done. Remember, if you want to apologize at our next meeting, just contact Dan Foyt. His contact information is on the whiteboard behind me. And thank you, Susan, for bringing the cookies and coffee, as usual. Susan tells me that next month we'll have cupcakes with red, white, and blue sprinkles for the upcoming holiday. These will be donated by Petro Bakery, so thank you, Les! Have a good evening, all, and see you next month, on July 1. Meeting adjourned!

(sound of gavel)

(Submitted by Dan Foyt, Secretary, June 1, 2019)

CALLINGS

MARIAN KELLY

What do you feel called to do?
Listen to the stirrings inside,
but pay attention:
which voices are calling to you?

Fear, outrage, and lament
will prompt you down paths
with ends
too readily foreseen.

Lift your head higher than these,
plant your feet deeper than these,
and listen again.

Look at the world in front of you,
breathe the air around you,
and once more
listen.

Trees and stones,
mighty in their quiet doings,
will never lie to you.

Frogs and rivers
with their symphonies of sound
will sing you only truth.

There is solace
in the simple act
of lifting your eyes to the sky.

There is magic
everywhere
in every moment
in all of the tiniest happenings
that you can imagine.

DEATHWATCH

LOUISE THAYER

For Lisa.

I knew there would be too many people.
I didn't know exactly why though,
until I watched them
from my corner of the floor.

I sandwiched myself next to the dog kennel with its four,
born-new puppies
squirming as I used them for an occasional excuse to take my
eyes off you.

I hadn't wanted to see you
dying
until the phone call
told me that it was going to be this weekend.

Even if I had known it was happening soon,
I probably wouldn't have visited before now,
preferring instead to remember the last time we rode thirty
miles together.

Not that long ago, you were our trail boss, so efficient,
locating where we should go and not
get lost amongst the rocks and Cholla cacti we were nee-
dle-threading through.

I wanted the pristine memory of us that night in the camp-
ground,
your motor home full with the sound of schoolgirl laughter,
though I was the youngest one there.

Peggy, at 83, had warned us most ferociously
not to step on her head
if we had to get up in the night to pee.
For some reason
Gail and I, comfortably squashed in the bunk above, had been
amused
beyond control, starting the giggling that went on for the next
half an hour.
You, in the middle, joined in once you had finished your long
undressing.

When I first came to know you,
I saw enough
about the thinness of your hair,
and your cheekbones and color showed me what was going on
beneath your skin.

You told me everything yourself because on our frequent road
trips I saw
your bra stuffed with what looked like cheap padding to cover
the side that had been slashed and shunted too many times for
no permanent gain.

I felt sad you hadn't been reconstructed, but you didn't care about that,
although the fact that your hand sometimes seized up did matter to you.
And so, when you couldn't pull on the zipper, I helped to yank and pin you into complicated outfits before I ever
put on my own.

I learned that otherwise you would become peevish,
like a child,
throwing objects or insults at others
in a short-lived rage that came from deep.
It wasn't at all a selfless act, though you probably thought it so.

The best and the worst turned out,
and it was easy to discern who,
amongst the many gathered around your small frame,
was there more for themselves and not for you.

This time I was in the middle,
knowing that why I came
was not so much to be there for you,
but to be there for me.

Your passing didn't scare me because it was overdue in a way
that I didn't understand until I saw your readiness to let go.
But death still had a hold on me
and I needed to see it at work.

It turns out there was no big mystery,
just your breath softly catching, pausing, and restarting
each time with a collective intake
from the room as we held fast
our own exhalations
to hear if this would be your last.

The laughing, talking, and singing were fine because you may
have been able to hear,
but I hated the greed in the eyes
of the people who wanted to claim you
as a story for Monday.

I couldn't stay until the end,
not because I couldn't face it,
but because I had horses
to feed.
I knew you
would have understood.

AWAKEN

LAUREN WOODBRIDGE

I awaken with a start and race out to the fields, the sound of
thunder crackles through my core.

I feel the moisture in the soil as mud coils through my toes.

The thought of young shoots growing fills me
with a desperate bliss.

I take a deep breath in expecting something pure, but the dust
sends me reeling and my dread begins to grow.

With deepest pain the truth begins to dawn. The crack of
thunder is nothing more than my heart breaking once again.

The mud around my toes, just my blood, sweat and tears
poured into barren soils with all my heart and soul.

A determined grimace cracks my parched lips as I begin
another day, marching in a war that has no end in sight.

LIZZY

JOANNA SAVAGE COLEMAN

Lizzy tells me she is only thirty.
She has a secret, she tells me,
she hasn't told anyone before.
Not even her sister.
Lizzy is afraid of her husband.
Sometimes he beats her.
Sometimes, even the children.

She glances to where my name tag hangs,
as though she hasn't met me one hundred times before.
Lizzy asks me where her shoes are.
It's getting dark outside and she should be getting home.
She tells me her husband will be angry.

Lizzy is covered in sores;
the kind that gets infected,
and her body has given up on trying to heal.
Her eyelids hang red and raw.
There's fermented skin,
where her fingernails once were.

Lizzy lives in room 201.

At breakfast, she asks me when her husband will be coming.
He visits every afternoon.
He brings her candy,
years of pain, scribbled over his face.
His dedication is enormous.
His love for his wife is a whisper;
he'll never say goodbye.
He simply tells her he needs to use the bathroom, then leaves,
punching the security-code into the worn-out
keypad by the doors.

Once he's gone,
Lizzy asks me when her husband will be coming.
I tell her he will be here soon,
and if not today then tomorrow.
He works on the farm, she tells me.
He'll feed the dogs when he gets back.
She tells me he's very busy,
and he's a good man,
but it's getting dark outside and she should be getting home.
She tells me her husband will be angry.

It would seem some fears can follow you to safety.
I don't know who Lizzy is afraid of:
The stooped and broken man, who brings her candies every
day at four?
Shuffling up the halls,
his frame, folded then unfolded, like a crumpled paper-boat
over his walking-cane?
Or is it some past lover, long since past?
I could ask her,
but it's too late now and she won't remember.

Lizzy picks at her skin and doesn't understand why there's all
this blood on her hands.
She unfurls her bandages methodically,
folding them neat, like laundry, on the seats next to her.
Lizzie's children have their own grandchildren now,
but Lizzy tells me she is only thirty.
How could she know the men, twice her age,
who call her 'Mother' when they visit with her?

She asks me where her shoes are,
but Lizzy can't walk anymore.

She asks me how long she'll be staying here,
and I tell her it's just until she gets better.
Lizzy holds my hand and thanks me for listening to her.
For a brief moment, there's this feeling of peace around her.

Then she asks me where her shoes are.

It's getting dark outside and she should be getting home.
She tells me her husband will be angry.

MILK AND SUGAR

ANN LEVY

I tap my foot, impatiently waiting for the old man in line ahead of me to find his money. He's slapping each of his pockets, smiling apologetically at the cashier all the while.

After the awful week Chet's had, I want to treat my still slumbering sweetie to a special breakfast of cinnamon buns, eggs, bacon, and fresh coffee. After I pop the buns in the oven, I walk to this convenience store for the rest of the supplies. On the way I list what I need to buy. Let's see, there's eggs, bacon, coffee. I have milk.

And here I stand, stuck in line with my arms full of groceries. I glance up. The man has found his wallet and is counting out change, penny by penny. Glaciers move faster, I think. I roll my eyes and try to distract myself by planning my next steps. Pay for this stuff, then run back home before the buns burn. Chet won't even know I was gone. I'll be back on track to making a meal fit for a king.

I appraise the situation. I could be here a while yet. I try to feel sympathy for the man, try to imagine him as somebody's grandfather. It's not easy; I feel mounting anger instead. He finally finishes and turns. "Have a good morning, young lady!" he tells me. Young? I snort with laughter and wiggle my fingers at him. He waves back and then shuffles to the door. I hear it ding behind him as I dump my choices on the counter. I feel someone come up too close beside me, and then I see a gun barrel pointed over my shoulder at the cashier. "Stop what you're doing. Give me all your Enfamil!"

Enfamil? Why would anyone steal Enfamil? Where's the baby?

I turn around to stare at the gunman. It's a young man, looking like he hasn't slept in a decade or two. Right after the last time he washed his hair. My heart goes out to him. I want to make him tea, offer to hold the baby for him, send him to bed for a nap. The cashier, hands in the air, gestures to the key ring beside the register. "I need to unlock it", she squeaks.

What? Oh, yeah. They lock up formula now. It's in the case behind the register. I look at him again, seeing reality this time. This child has a gun, and isn't sweet and tired, but strung out and desperate. Probably a thug, high on something. I wonder if the cashier hit the silent alarm, like on TV. I glance to the side, looking for signs of an off-duty undercover cop lurking around the dairy section, planning our rescue. No such savior exists.

Damn, why did I decide to come here? I could've got in the car and driven to that new store; it's not far! But, no, I had to try to make it here and back before Chet came downstairs. I think back to what I left at the house. I've got those cinnamon buns in the oven, they'll probably burn to a crisp before this craziness plays out. I only had like 20 minutes.

I shake my head in disgust. Let them burn! Buns aren't my main worry, now. I look back at the gunman, now directing the cashier to unlock the case. My mind races in outrage. Guess you couldn't have waited two minutes, until I'd left, huh? I was the only person in here! You'd have had the whole place to yourself. But NO! Bet you're not good at waiting. Bet it's always about you, isn't it? Bet you don't think about anything but yourself and what you want. And now you're making that poor baby pay for your ego.

The bell over the door dings. It's some young, strong guy. He'll run back outside as soon as he sees us frozen in fear at the register. But he doesn't. It's a sweaty jogger, just out of the park, still red in the face. All he's thinking about is a drink; maybe water, or one of those vitamin infusions. Head down, he darts toward the back of the store, making for the glass coolers. He never sees the tableau in front of the register; the scared old lady in her hoodie, the gunman, the cashier with the can of Enfamil in one hand, a key ring in the other. He's more interested in his watch. Oh, great, now he's looking at his phone.

Dial 911!

Dial 911!

Dial 911!

I try to command the runner with my mind, like that Jedi Mind Trick from Star Wars. But no luck; he's probably checking his fitness app. We're on our own, looks like. If the runner hasn't noticed the gunman, the gunman notices him. He yells from the register, "Hey you! Freeze! Drop that phone!"

The runner's head snaps up, a look of anger at being so rudely treated, a retort on his lips. Then his color rapidly goes from red to deathly pale. His eyes widen, and his mouth snaps shut. Wow, your eyes really do roll back in your head when you faint, I think. The runner collapses to the floor in the aisle leading back to the coolers. We all hear the "thunk" as his head hits the tiles.

The next few things happen in a blur. The gunman crumples with an "OOF!" The cashier holds the heavy can of formula over her head triumphantly, menacingly. I frantically dig in my pocket and pull out my phone. I unlock it and dial 911. My heart is thumping; I can't breathe. I might throw up. I swallow once, twice. No, I'm okay. I take another breath. Yeah, I confirm to myself. The runner wakes up, flops over to his stomach, and rolls his head to the side to lay his cheek against the cold tile.

Why isn't my call going through? I look at my phone in exasperation. Shit! I left it on all night. The battery's dead. I must get the runner's phone. But first I move cautiously over to the gunman to disarm him. The cashier, understanding my motive, kicks the gun. It skitters down an aisle. She is still holding the can of Enfamil like a weapon. Once we're both sure the robber is out cold, she nods at me with one of the most satisfied looks I've ever seen. Then she looks back down at him.

The bell on the door dings again. "Rob? The baby finally fell asleep. She wasn't hungry after all. I brought your wallet, you forgot it in the car. Better get the formula, and more diapers before she wakes up. And grab some food for us, OK?" It's a young woman, looking exhausted and desperate.

The runner finds his voice. He jumps to his feet. I wonder if maybe he shouldn't stand up so fast, but don't say anything. "Rob's going down, and you're going with him, so don't even think it!" he screams. The girl snaps a look at the runner and then whirls to look at us at the register.

"Rob! Rob?" Her head whips around again to the runner. "Don't even think what? What are you talking about?" She turns on the cashier and me. "Wha--? What did you do to him? I have a sleeping baby in the car!" Girl-Mom is confused, scared, enraged, and yelling at the top of her lungs.

Before the cashier can answer, the runner runs to find the gun down the aisle. I yell at Girl-Mom that Rob is out cold, and that when he wakes up, the police are going to send him straight to jail. She stops yelling, and stares at me in shock. "Rob? Going to jail? What for? The baby's been up all night, crying, and we haven't slept for two days! We ran out of formula and we're almost out of diapers! I just want a shower, some breakfast, and for her to shut up!" Suddenly she's crying.

Recognizing the signs of a mother on the edge, I backpedal furiously. "Let him go!" I hiss to the cashier.

The runner comes up to the register, a dazed but relieved

look on his face. "This gun is a toy." I look over and recognize it from the Toys "R" Us ads. It's a six-shooter from The Cowboy Collection. The only way that Rob could hurt us with it would be if he'd thrown it at us.

I turn back to Girl-Mom, whose outrage is gathering steam as her tears dry up. I shout, "Rob was trying to hold us up with a pretend gun to get Enfamil. We thought he was going to shoot us. I almost threw up. I didn't call the police." I stop, trying to remember if I've covered the salient points of the morning so far. Girl-Mom starts to cry again. From a car parked outside in the parking lot come thin, distant wails.

"Aww, how old is your baby?" I ask. At the same time the runner says to the cashier "God, listen to the lungs on that one!"

"It's the only way she can communicate!" Girl-Mom and I are united in our defense of the crying baby. Rob, waking up on the floor, groans. "Oh, sweetheart!" Girl-Mom says. Her head whips around as she directs a glare to us all.

Well, that decides it. She's overwhelmed. I should take over before things get weird; or at least weirder.

I help Rob stand up, and he apologizes to the cashier and the runner. The cashier, just happy that her shift is almost over, nods silently. The runner says, "Oh, you're sorry? And that's supposed to make it all fucking okay?" Rob offers him a conciliatory candy bar from beside the register. The cashier promises to get him some ice from the freezer case for the bump on his head. He waves it off.

I ask him, "You sure? You fell hard when you fainted!" His eyes widen as he glares at me. He is suddenly eager to cover up his presence here today. He makes a noise of disgust, a "Lady, it's your funeral" snort and grabs the candy bar. The bell on the door dings with disapproval as he leaves.

I say briskly, "No harm, no foul. What sort of diapers do you use?" Girl-Mom looks at me wordlessly for a moment, then sprints to the car and her crying baby. Rob turns and sprints down the baby aisle. He reappears moments later with a bag of Pampers Cruisers.

"This is all together. I'm paying for them, too. The formula and the diapers", I tell the cashier. She starts to ring up all my purchases. We turn to walk outside. It's been a while since I had a young baby in the house, so I invite Girl-Mom and Rob home for breakfast, maybe a nap, and mothering of my own. Chet loves babies. Maybe we'll befriend them and get to take her to the park on weekends. That'd be nice, right?

"We might have cinnamon buns." I tell Rob. He nods, still dazed.

BUSY

LAUREN WOODBRIDGE

The phone rings. I answer it, voice peppy and light.

"Yes, I can talk that is fine. I have a spare 5 minutes of time."

I continue my work, hands busy, mind sharp.

The phone rings, work stops. "Yes, I can talk, it's no chore, no, I would never think you a bore."

Back to task at hand, refocus, there is work to be done.

The phone rings, "Yes I can, that is fine, I can help you anytime."

Try to find where I was, getting started once again.

My child calls, "Mummy can we play?"

The phone rings and as I answer it once again. I hear myself say, "Sorry kiddo, I'm busy, not today."

TO THE MEN WHO TRIED TO LOVE ME

LOUISE THAYER

I'm sorry
but I tried to love you too.

We worked hard to pretend
to each other that we knew
what lay below
the cover of our lives.

Ever floating behind
pretty willing eyes,
I let you rescue me
whenever you thought
that's what I needed,
until I wanted
to save myself
from the lies
I didn't know that we'd believed.

I am dark and dirt
and how I always should have been.

Fertile with the knowledge
I am mine-deep
and dangerous when hurt.

I am pressed against the pores
of my own skin from inside
and I seep through my body
from worm-ridden holes,
substrate for my soul,
until a garden erupts
from within.

When you thought that you loved me
you loved only what I seemed.

Teeming now, life-full, I pour forth
past your expectations
and lack of time
to dream.

I am mine.

Deep and darkly
sorry.

Me.

MAY 15TH

ALYSSA REVELS

I didn't cry for you, this year.
The anniversary came and went
And only your song,
Our song,
Made me check what day it was.
I'm not sure why I missed it—
Maybe it was endless work
And papers to grade.
Maybe it was motherhood
And chasing sticky soft fingers everywhere.
It's not that I don't miss you.
No,
The sorrow creeps in like the tide
Until I'm unmoored and adrift
Whether in seawater or salty tears—no difference.
I dream of what could have been.
Of little curls and rosy cheeks.
A due date left undone.
I didn't cry for you, this year.
But, my daughter, I love you.

THE NOTE I FOUND IN A JAR

KIRSTEN ELIZABETH YEAGER

For my Brother, Danny

The note l found in a jar:
Your pick,
So surprised by it
To think that you held it
Between your fingers
As I held it in mine.
Looking for your prints
Not seeing any
But feeling them
With all my soul.
Nicked deep with songs
I know we sang together
Sometime,
A long time ago.
I'd like to know the song
You sang
With that pick
Between your fingers
The very last time.

And now it's mine.
And I wish it wasn't.
I miss your songs,
And your crazy ideas,
And your laughter,
And just you,
Just you.
Who you were,
And how you made me
Who I was.
And how I'm not sure now
Who I am
Without you.

SMELLING THE BEST

MARY MCGINNIS

Sit with me—
may you love my no-flower,
every-inch-a-woman smell, my
light-as-air-hair smell, my minus-
lilac smell;
I offer my wrist: it's
never been tattooed. It's a
good wrist, broken at
the age of six, but it healed.
Here are my eyebrows, never plucked or penciled;
but they're my eye-
brows, not very hairy but so what?
My eyes are partly closed but they can
Shine, sometimes. I may
touch your hand. I don't know who you are.

VOICES OF NATURE

By discovering nature, you discover yourself.

Maxime Lagacé

YOUNG PUP

TESSA PAGONES

My dogs have come into my life at different ages (theirs, not mine, though mine too, as I have acquired them over the course of many years). I do not consider myself a dog person. I came to dogs later in life, and I hope I have evolved over time into a better dog owner. I was used to cats and a particular level of self-sufficiency and independence. Dogs can be self-sufficient and independent too, but it's pretty irresponsible to let them just roam. I know that better now, but when my first dog would disappear from the yard for hours on end, I didn't worry about it nearly as much as I should have—enough to stop it from happening again, for instance.

Her wandering led to some amusing stories. The time, for instance, that she came home and had clearly been swimming in the neighbor's pool one hot summer day. Or the fish filets she used to bring home and eat in the yard. I never did figure out if she was going through someone's trash or if she was stealing someone's dinner they had set out to defrost on the deck rail. And then there was the time I had a feeling she had headed to the road, so I was walking down the driveway to look for her when a car pulled in, the back door opened, and my dog got out.

All of these are a lot like stories from my own younger days: they are funny to relate now, but as a grown up and as a parent, I am mildly horrified even at my own stories. I know some of my children's stories, and I'm sure there are others they will tell me at some point in the distant future, and others they will never let me know about.

This week is the two-year anniversary of the arrival of my youngest dog. Dogs, at least my dogs, seem to be the opposite of children in photograph quantity. Anyone who is a youngest child is familiar with the albums of photos of their siblings, especially the oldest, and the dearth of photos chronicling their own milestones. I have probably one roll of film (remember rolls of film?) of my current old dog in his first two years with us, and approximately 753,000 digital photos of the youngest one. Part of that is due to available technology, and part of it represents the different level of attention I give my dogs now.

This week is also the week my oldest child is moving away from home. My kids also came into my life at different ages (theirs, not mine—unlike the dogs I got all three kids at once). My youngest is now four years older than I was when I first met them. I suppose at this point saying "I'm not a dog person" is a lot like saying "I'm not a mother." I may not have started out envisioning a life full of dogs and kids, but sometimes you get what you expect and sometimes you get lucky.

There have been a lot of milestones for my kids since the beginning of the dog years. Graduations, engagements, break-ups, marriage, first job, first more-grown-up-than-mine job, house purchases, house sale. They have all moved out of our house. One has moved out of the state. Two have moved back into our house. The oldest is now leaving our house again, and moving far away.

They get older and they do their own thing and they express themselves and their independence in their own ways. With each new step, I cheer them on and I'm excited for the next chapter in their lives and a part of me thinks "it's about time" and gives them a little shove out of the nest.

But then there's this other part. The part that sees the U-Haul my oldest child has rented to move 1,700 miles away sitting in the driveway as he begins to load up his stuff. The part of me that flashes back instantly to the first time I met him, when he was seven years old, telling me in great detail about his math homework, with his bowl haircut and his fashion sense and his extensive vocabulary. It's the same part of me that spoke at my middle child's wedding, when all I could remember was him at age three, fearlessly throwing himself at everything life put in his path, but wearing a helmet and knee and elbow pads just in case, because you never know when you might need a little protection. It's the same part of me that sees my youngest child being more adult than I feel like I will ever be in her job and relationship and living space decisions and yet I hear her deep toddler voice chanting "Hode you mommy hode you mommy hode you mommy" when she wanted to be picked up and carried.

No matter how old or young they are when they take these big steps in their lives, no matter how ready they are, no matter how ready I am, I'm not ready. I still look at the adults they are and see the kids they were, and I want to reach out past the U-Haul and snatch them back and make the time I wanted to go faster go just a little more slowly.

FIRST FIRE

ELIZABETH LOVE KENNON

Winter came stealing round the house last night, not ready to make a commitment, just looking for a one-night stand; hoping to cheat Autumn out of one of our last evenings together. He can be like that, you know.

Autumn is a lush, and I adore her. She woos me with reds and yellows, draping her gemstones from the trees, just to see me smile. No gesture is too grand. She lavishes her table with thick stews, pies, and mulled wine. Everyone is invited, but we sneak out when no one's looking, and get drunk on the sweet clear air, and the long golden embrace of the late afternoon sun. Each time she comes around, I dream of running off together in gypsy shawls, following her past the line of birds to the edge of the horizon.

But last night, Winter crashed the party. I left the windows closed, not ready for him yet, and woke to twenty degrees, and a hard frost scattered across the yard; crystals clinging to the glass, angry petals, left by a temperamental lover—part threat, part promise. Fierce and moody, he's impatient with Autumn's hedonism. He has his own agenda, his own way. Of course, when he's done, he marches off without so much as a goodbye. But you can't take that personally. That's just him. And between you and me, we're both ready to part ways by then.

With a growl, he sweeps away the last of the summer haze,

and paints Autumn's ambers and garnets in hues of gray: tree bark, frost on the fallow earth, low clouds rolling, smoke rising on the wind. Without adornment, and without fanfare, he courts. His intensity alone compels.

He's not a gentle lover—too demanding, no compromise. But he delights in juxtaposition, the pop and crackle of a fire, red embers glowing against the howl of wind outside. Everything comes clear in his company, and when I follow him, I find myself staring into deep pools along an unbeaten trail. His gifts are hard won. I come away from our bed richer, stronger, his fierceness seeping into my bones.

My pulse quickens as I light this first fire of the season. The wood smoke carries his scent back to me, and I'm ready to dance with him again: wood chips on the floor; silent morning walks; ice coating bare branches; and a night sky with stars so big, I reach up to pluck them.

I don't want to miss his call, so I light the fire, smoke trailing through the chimney; a signal that I'll be here.

Waiting.

To follow where he takes me.

EXCUSES IN DEER SEASON

KATE BREMER

Seriously! there is a chihuahua on my notebook—
now he's sitting on my wrist, trying to lick my glasses.
I wanted to write about burning flags and burying
my country, singing to my dead cat Muse, and
playing "Suzanne" over and over again on YouTube.

BUT, Dutch Apple is here reminding me that I
have dogs and donkeys to love, a mustang,
cats, an Io Moth caterpillar and Common
Mestra visitors. AND Sandhill cranes flying so close
I can see their toes and bills, rattling off to the
Bosque del Apache. Deer are in all the yards—

Sheltering from FrontPage—FirstKill—Toddler
Photos. Yesterday I started to bring
a poem out of a burning flag and the stillness
of horses, but at just that moment, Cinderella
blasted the loudest donkey fart ever. I don't
even like to write the word: "fart". Those animals
must be eating flags, deer blood, Jesus's shroud
and Buddha's relics. I can't help but laugh—

And take my poem out of the goat's mouth,
out of the coyote trap, out of the mass
of frog eggs in the stock tank, Out
of the Super Moon rays and off of the belly
of the black-eyed begging Chihuahua.

DONKEY DOWN

LINDA DOUGHTY

We walked down the hill to the neighbor's house.
We were going to see if we could help get Rosie back up.
She'd slipped in the muck that
the desert rains had left behind,
her right side pressed flat,
right foreleg pinned under;
she struggled once to get up, almost made it,
then sank again.

Four gray mares,
one a happy sorrel appy-dappled across her back
from memories and ill-fitting saddles,
curious and unhindered and now.

Three aging mare-women:
Rosie's owner wiry and white-haired,
tiny and mighty,
sharp blue eyes made sharper by
underlying tears.

Three brawny guys tagged along,
one carrying a halter. Ever so gently he put it on her.
Mama Rosie had no fight left.
We lifted her part way, and I pulled her right leg free,
so that both front hooves rested on drying mud canyons.

Lightly.

We struggled against her heaviness,
then let her rest.
Her eyes showed no pain.
Nystagmus.

We lifted her head, removed her halter,
then put a clean towel under to shield her eye.
I adjusted her ears for comfort.
"I could call Hank and have him shoot her, I guess. The vet was
here three days ago and said we might have to put her down."
"If you know how to do it right, that could be okay."
"Last time, when he put Mercy's mare down, he had to shoot
her three times."
"Call the vet" I said.
Mama Rosie's son looked on.

I saved my tears for the walk back up the hill.

THAT SATURDAY

LASELL JARETZKI BARTLETT

Saturday morning, we went out to the barn to feed. I was letting the guinea fowl out of their pen and Terry was checking on the horses, Rusty and Sam, and their hay bags and water.

Terry yelled to me. I looked to where he stood in the run-in shed, noticed Sam standing next to him, and after a moment barely made out an awkward dark mass in the shadows of the shed. Rusty was down, on the ground, at a time when he shouldn't be.

I heard Terry yell, "Rusty has passed!" I took some steps, eyes widening in the beginnings of shock and narrowing in hopes of better seeing what was in the shed. Instant flashbacks flooded me from two previous times I found beloved horses dying when we went out for morning chores. I was stunned, and moving toward Terry I called out, "What?"

Terry yelled again, "Rusty is cast. He's cast!" This sunk in enough to get me running. I came through the gate as quickly as I could and finally close enough, saw Rusty lying upside down, eyes rolling, groaning, head extended and teeth gnawing at the shed wall, little else in motion. I was horrified, not knowing how long he'd been stuck, not knowing if he was going to survive this.

Despite my horror and shock, I moved into action. I told Terry, "I'm getting ropes," and I told Rusty, "We're going to help you. I'll be right back," before sprinting to the tack room. I grabbed the longest two ropes I could find knowing we'd want some distance from flailing hooves, assuming Rusty would attempt to get up. I sprinted back to the run-in shed.

I handed one rope to Terry as I placed the other around Rusty's near front leg. Terry handed me a length of the second rope which I put around Rusty's near hind leg. Terry said, "Put it around both legs," so I did. Then I put the first rope around both front legs. Rusty curled his head up off the ground as I was doing this and conveniently hooked his neck into the loop of rope as well, as if to help us help him.

Together Terry and I hauled on the ropes. "One, two, three, pull!" We shifted Rusty a little. We hauled again, and released, and hauled and released, rocking his body like when your car is stuck in snow and you have to get it rocking to get unstuck. Then we got him past the tipping point away from the wall and scrambled back out of the way while he got up, blew some air, and walked over to a hay net and started eating.

When I saw Rusty up and moving, I sank to my knees. My heart rate was off the charts from sprinting, and from the effort to roll Rusty over. Also, my heart was pounding from the adrenaline rush of angst that came when I thought Rusty might have been cast for long enough to be dying.

I stayed there, leaning on one arm while pressing on my pounding heart with my free hand. I was breathing hard at maximum imaginable capacity, and letting my body make sounds that matched my fear and my exertion.

Terry had come to stand by me and put his hand on my shoulder, asking if I was okay. I leaned into our contact. I was okay. At least I was pretty sure I was okay although my heart kept pounding with worrisome force. I kept pressing on my heart with my hand.

As things started to settle, I wrapped my arms around myself and let my curiosity grow about this arousal and settling process. I could breathe easily again, and my heart rate was slowing down. I could see Rusty looking like nothing had happened, not dull or disoriented from being in shock, nor unsteady on his feet. He was okay. I was okay. We all were okay.

Except Sam. He had been startled and alarmed by my dash to the shed with two long ropes flopping in my arms. He was running back and forth in the next paddock, fleeing in fear caused by my unusual behavior and unusually loud upset sounds.

I got up, walked to where he could see me, and spoke to him in my more familiar calm tone of voice. He came to a stop, eyes still wide with uncertainty, then approached me cautiously, sniffed my offered hand, and took a deep breath, exhaling much of his tension. Now Sam was okay, too.

Terry hung out with Sam while I hung out with more of my settling process. Rusty hung out with the hay.

What was remarkable to me was that I didn't freeze and collapse even though part of me went into shock when I was first aware of this potentially life-threatening horse crisis. I knew we needed ropes and I went for them. Also remarkable was how intense my physiology became, how easily I could be with it, and how quickly things started to settle after such a huge arousal.

Occasionally through the day I thought back to what had happened. I felt relieved that Terry and I were able to move Rusty's thousand-pound body. I marveled that Rusty appeared so normal so quickly with no signs of the physiological collapse that can happen when a horse (or any mammal) is stuck—unable to flee or fight in order to survive—and slips into the immobility of shock. I worried that his apparently normal behavior was covering some internal injuries.

I was deeply grateful that Terry was there with me offering physical assistance and emotional support. I wasn't alone in this crisis.

I had several episodes of feeling inundated by waves of heartache. This situation reminded me of how helpless we can feel when a beloved is in trouble, even as we take action to save them. This situation reminded me of how vulnerable horses are, even though they are big and powerful, adaptable and resilient in their own horsey ways. This situation reminded me of the near-death experiences in my life when I had been stuck, unable to flee or fight, unaided and alone, and had gone into the immobility of shock.

I love this horse deeply. My heart expands with warmth when I think of Rusty and our years together. My heart aches with sorrow when I imagine life without him.

That evening while Rusty was eating, I brought my attention with heightened awareness to smelling him, touching him, listening to his chewing, feeling his warmth, his breathing, his winter coat, his muscles and bones—being with and being touched by the dimensions of his special Rusty-ness.

Although we can't capture these moments as easily as taking a photograph with a camera, I do have this rich blend of memories—sensory and visual, kinesthetic and energetic. And these are mine forever.

THE RULEBREAKER

KATE BREMER

For Cinderella: Writing with the Humans*

Talking stick, she stands in front of each reader,
Her warm wall of safety—my kind of barricade—
Earthen, furry, and long-eared.

Rearranging things—a purse, a rattle—
Untying a steel-toed boot. She'd
Like her own drum, a little bell to ring—
Enchanting us. Appreciated, admired,
Beautiful black burro. No dissembling—just wild
Rose, centipede, Ashe juniper,
Eastern phoebe, Carolina chickadee. Stand in
A sunset for at least ten minutes, moon into marrow,
Kitchen window donkey. Sync your cells with acorn,
Elevate the woodland jay and wheels of pollen—
Remember winter tadpoles and THE RULEBREAKER.

*I host a monthly get-together on my property called Writing and
Drumming with the Herd. Cinderella, one of my sassiest donkeys,
is very involved in the process.

AMONG THE HORSES

CHRIS KENT

The young girl slips through the barbed wire fencing, a slight ripping sound occurs as her thin cotton dress -the one with red cherries intertwined with green leaves- gets caught on the barbs. A worried look passes fleetingly across her face. She shrugs and wipes the ditch mud from her shoe where she misjudged her jump across.

The sun dapples through swaying trees. The hill rises in front of her and there, spread out, her horses are grazing quietly. Well not exactly her horses, but hers for the short time she is here, and in her continued imagination and dreams. She comes here every day she can while she is holidaying. This morning she rose at dawn and crept out of the little holiday chalet her family shared (there will be a huge argument about that later).

The horses turn their heads, one gently whickers a soft call in her direction. Her heart fills. Quiet excitement builds. She approaches him. His name is Leprechaun and he is a smoky grey colour. She strokes his gleaming mane and his soft warm coat. She quietly goes to see each horse before sitting on the log in her own secret shady hollow. The air is heavy with the scent and sounds of endless summer. Flies buzz lazily, birds sing and swoop.

The horses' breath is grass sweet on her face. Restful, calming. One by one they slowly come over, and rest by her.

Lowering their necks and arching their heavy heads over hers, closing their eyes into a deep dreaming sleep. She waves the flies away from their eyes.

The endless blue sky overhead is her ceiling. Cool mossy grass and leaves her floor. The trees offer shade, shelter, and invisibility. She feels a sense of completeness and peace.

As an only child these holidays are part fun, part torture. She reads, swims when she can, and takes refuge from parental and family conflict. Avoids the strange alleged faith healer in the adjoining chalet that her aunt obviously rather likes, and who makes her own skin prickle and crawl. She retreats into her books, and this sacred field. Her log is comfortable, the horses seem content to graze and doze close by. She feels connected by an invisible thread as she sees their eyelids droop and feels their breath deepen. She matches their breathing, slow and deep. Their hearts beat in time. A muted but powerful joy, excitement, connection, and peace floods her heart.

Hours pass.

She has a natural reluctance to be seen, it is after all, a secret. At 10 years old, secrets are best kept guarded. This day she gets a little too casual, a little too relaxed. The Horse Girls, as she calls them, come marching over the top of the hill. They look tall and imposing, full of confidence and power. Their long hair snapping in the wind, leather boots creaking, head collars jangling across their grownup shoulders. Before she can run, they are in front of her. She has finally been caught, napping.

Did she not know that horses can be dangerous? They kick, and bite, and can tread on people. It was private land and she had no right to be there.

She cries. Partly feeling ashamed but mostly knowing that her dream times are over, and her secret sanctuary has been discovered. She loses track of the conversation, already scheming of ways to still visit without getting caught out again.

The Main Horse Girl is asking her if she was listening.

She nods yes.

The Main Horse Girl repeats "If you want to, come to the stables, you can do some jobs, and we can maybe let you ride? Would you like that?"

Ride? you mean actually sit on one of these magnificent creatures, be able to spend holiday times with them without worrying about getting caught? To be with them without hiding? To become a Horse Girl, even if a small one. Relief washes over her. She feels a bit giddy.

"Get your parents to bring you, but don't let us catch you in here again!"

The Horse Girls look at each other sideways, small smiles flash across their lips. They knew they would catch up with her, eventually. They recognized her small girl dreams, her need to be among the horses. The Horse Girls Knew.

Dreams not quite crushed, a chance to know these horses more, to maybe even ride. To feel free, and to be carried by a being so magnificent. She could not believe her luck. Her soul filled with hope.

That was the beginning of the transformation of horses from the safe, secret, and sacred, to a constantly changing list of do's and don'ts; to pages of how's and how not's; to lessons in why's and why nots. And wherefores. Always plenty of wherefores.

Many years later, sitting under the willow tree she shares with her little herd, she wonders how come it took so damn long to get back to that childhood wonder and simple grace.

WYOMING SUITE

SARAH BARNES

I: Elk Must Move Deliberately Through Dense Woods

Watching the big male watch me,
Antlers spanning the full width of the clearing
Through which we have glimpsed one another,
I hold completely still,
Afraid that seeing me, he might bound away.

Instead, he stands a moment,
Bestowing on me the honor of his majestic gaze,
Then takes his time to turn about,
Continuing his stately progress through the forest,
Regardless of my presence or desire for him to stay.

Only after he has gone does it occur to me
His measured pace reflects not so much concern for his own
dignity,
Nor yet complete indifference to my being there,
As the need for a creature with antlers the size of his
To thread a careful path through close-growing trees.

Still, it is his gift of noblesse oblige that remains with me
Even after he has gone upon his deliberate royal way.

II: Without a Map

Wandering, I follow a woodland trail,
unconcerned as to its destination.
Whatever is beyond the next shaded
bend is not waiting for me.
Nor am I hoping to find anything in
particular when I get there.

Chipmunks, chasing round the solid trunk of an obliging tree,
Pause only briefly amid the pine boughs to scold my passing
Before resuming their essential business.

The forest, though not unaware,
is blessedly indifferent to my presence.
Nothing here depends on me, nor is anything required,
Beyond noticing where along the path I place my feet.

The wanderer must be me, not lost,
but relieved of any expectation
Of knowing the way I am supposed to go.

III: Along the Snake

Peace is a river, flowing quietly past a thick stand of reeds
That tremble in conversation with a gentle wind.

Here infinite beauty coalesces in the iridescent blue flash
Of dragonfly wings.

And the earth's tremendous mystery resides in one leaf,
swirling idly,
Carried by the languid current.

HERITAGE

CRISSI MCDONALD

On a Smoky Mountain ridge
between boulders honed like knives,
you, rare Spruce tree,
raced erosion
in time measured by growth rings.
Through centuries you've stood,
shelter for birdsong,
making music with the wind.
Your roots
chased rain through
a maze of loose rock.
You started small and pliable;
though singular in your existence
the forest stood sentinel in its
subterranean plurality
while seasons shaped trunk and limbs,
and under your bark,
rings spun out
in wavy thin ripples.
You fell during the squall
of a far north hurricane
the plummet
of your body

echoing off ridges
the storm rearranged.
Now, lying in dirt,
your trunk a
squamation of dents,
your roots exposed and
sluicing rain
from a sky your branches
can no longer reach for,
As you slumbered toward death with
days and stars passing over you
did you know?
Did you know
while your old form
lay withering there was
a new life, cocooned within your skin?
(phloem, cambium, xylem)
Did you hear echoed in
people's voices that bounced from the cliffs
the promise of the
resurrection of your own?

Did the wind carry
future plucked notes,
vibrato in four time?
Did you know that the birds
whose song garlanded
your branches
would transform into hands?
First, the hands with centuries honed
skill that shaped you
into a guitar,
wide-hipped and throaty.
Then the hands
that coaxed rippling music

from your epoch-hardened skin.
The transformation from seed to sapling,
tree to music-giver: this heritage
spirals more deeply
than your roots ever could.

THE ROAD TO BUCK

KATE MCLAUGHLIN

No one told me how I was going to feel—to be sat with my own internal conflict, knowing that what I was doing is limited at best, and instinctively knowing that there must be another way. Self-ridicule and admonishment usually follow next, whilst I traverse through the different trainers out there trying to find something that fits. The internet is in its infancy, so google cannot help me. I ended up with that one horse that found me at a time where I should have felt that after all these years riding, studying, competing, and sweating, I am at least semi competent. Then that animal showed me that I didn't know very much at all.

I found myself fighting against the trend of equestrian mechanics and started to follow my gut when approaching how horses are be trained; the world of knowledge started to open up a little with the emergence of the 'World Wide Web' and a happenstance crossing of paths with those who are similarly minded and have had the courage to forge a new path and ask the question, "why?" I heard words like vaquero and classical dressage not really knowing what that is all about, even though I have devoured every book and physical resource I could since being a small girl first reading about horses and watching westerns with my mum in a tenement flat in Glasgow. Some wait for me to outgrow "that phase" and those people are still waiting.

Around 2002 I heard the name Buck Brannaman mentioned, but there wasn't enough information available for me to indulge my curiosity further, and looking back, I wasn't on that path yet ... I didn't even know what that path is. Over the next few years, I read all of Mark Rashid's work, and I whimsically watch the Horse Whisperer knowing that behind the movie making there is something real in that relationship with Pilgrim. I know because I have felt it with my own horse, every time I've been told to pull on the reins harder and add more leg, technically it may be correct to some, but something dies a little inside me as there must be another way. I then went on meet some natural horsemanship riders, and study some of Ken Faulkner's work, and for the first time felt supported and encouraged that there were people who also wanted to forge a different path with horses and have practical tools and techniques to build success. I then heard the names Tom Dorrance and Ray Hunt, and I started to dig a little deeper and what I discovered lead me straight back to Buck Brannaman—and that fanned the flame of knowledge further.

I am not a famous trainer but I have been on the road to better horsemanship for almost three decades, and I would like to share with you an introduction to the memoir of the journey that brought me to a place in my life where riding in the first UK clinic with Buck Brannaman was a pinnacle in not just my equestrian endeavours at that time, but also in my life. What started as a passion to be the best horseman I could for my horse's benefit developed into taking the broken parts of me and begin to rebuild myself from the inside out. You may wonder how spending time with Buck would spark this transformation in not just my horsemanship skills, my horse but also in me, well, spending time with someone who is truly authentic has a domino effect if you open yourself up and are vulnerable enough to experience the moment, with a cognitive nakedness that I won't deny took me by surprise and was difficult at times. Timing is everything with horses and life, and the timing of this clinic was a catalyst that stripped me back and reminded me exactly who I am.

So, let me tell you about the first two days of the UK clinic that propelled not only my horse's education, but galvanized in me something long forgotten.

Day 1

We are all unique, with stories to tell, and to each our reality is our own. We can both experience the same event and have a completely different recollection of it, along with feelings assigned to that reality.

Before I delve into the first day of Buck's clinic, I want to share with you a glimmer of my truth. Why for me this was about more than horsemanship. Apart from the loss of my father, this clinic was always going to be a turning point in my horsemanship career for me.

Eight years ago, I had to walk away from life as I knew it. My horse, my job, house,

everything. I was a well-educated professional, wife and mother who after several years of having her confidence and self-esteem eroded, walked away from a toxic marriage. No one knew that abuse had taken place, no one knew that I was repeatedly punished for having horses in my life, no one knew I had to make a choice because I wasn't sure if I could survive it any longer.

I didn't know if I'd ever have horses in my life again. It is who I am, so I felt bereft.

When I did ride again what shocked me the most was this constant, the absolute comfort and certainty of my confidence and skill with them, was shaken. You can see this, was far more than if I could take my horse to a Buck clinic, this was more about me having the faith in myself that I could go to Aintree and feel I belonged there as a horsewoman whilst being the partner I needed to be for Tuff.

On the first morning everyone was understandably nervous. I felt focused (although a bit sick) and set about warming up and getting Tuff used to the size of the crowd. Music played, and a party vibe buzz filled the morning air, it was a good atmosphere. It was even better when I had a few familiar, and not so familiar faces, come up to me and say they were rooting for us, and they had been reading my blog (gulp)!

Normally everyone would be mounted by the time Buck entered the arena at an H1 clinic, but due to the nerves Buck allowed us some more time on the ground with our horses before mounting. Surprisingly, I was first up in the saddle...

I have to say at this point, as soon as Buck entered the area, there was a collective figurative sigh of relief from the participants. I have never met someone with such a calming, solid energy as Buck. He was a joy to be around. We felt it, and so did the horses. That's what I believed helped my cowgirl spirit and we went on to have an absolutely fantastic first day.

Buck made us all feel at home, told us we were among friends and not to be shy. We set about various tasks, including long serpentines. Now these, Mr.T and I usually have down pat, but I think my hands and legs were possibly on a delay system, so when it came to asking questions, I found myself asking one I thought I wouldn't need to. Now the emphasis here isn't actually about what I asked Buck, it is the way he responded.

I asked Buck about what should I do as I felt completely out of time when helping Tuff with the hand on the reach across when performing the long serpentine; Buck rode right up to me, read my name badge, backed up (this was all fluid and seamless on a horse he'd been on less than a couple of hours) and said, "Well Kate....there will be times when you have your timing in sync, and then times when you feel like you've dropped the anchor." What I found so humble, so human, is that he took the time and the effort to read my name badge and address me by my name. Well what is so special about that I bet you're wondering? It is that simple act of respect, that acknowledgement of me (and indeed everyone Buck spoke to) as a person which spoke volumes about him. I knew before we began I would be in the presence of an exceptional horseman, I knew right then that I was also in the presence of an exceptional human being.

In that nanosecond I remembered we all have a cross to bear and our own emotional

baggage, be it hand luggage or cargo sized, but that I would be ok. I could be authentic, real, and that wouldn't be perceived as a weakness in this man's eyes, it would simply be my truth. As we all know, horses are nothing but authentic, and now, I appreciate what the comfort of being truly accepted feels like for them.

Day 2

Throughout the journey back to Aintree on the morning of day two, my brain was on a bitter diatribe loop.... I'd survived day one, I could just go home now couldn't I? I know that's not actually what I wanted to do, but my old best friend doubt had woken up bright and cheery. This was further exacerbated by how Tuff was; slightly tucked up and stressed from being in all night. I know this horse inside out, and as soon as he had his halter on, he let down somewhat, but the wheel of perpetual self-doubt was in full swing. My emotional state fuelled his, and he went down to the arena like Seabiscuit. He was obedient, and to anyone else he probably looked fine, but I could feel every bit of insecurity course through him, straight back into me like a circuit. By the time we were in the arena and warming up, it all felt too much for me. I quietly warmed up and as we worked around the arena, I came across fellow participant Ann who took one look at me and said, "Are you ok?"

I confessed to Ann that it was all feeling a bit too much this morning. Ann reassured me we all felt the same. Wow did that make me feel better. Ann then encouraged me to go and tell Buck how I felt. "What??" My brain was screaming. "Go speak to Buck when I look like I'm emotionally unhinged!? Are you serious?"

At that moment Buck walked into the arena, and I tried to pull myself together. Ann turned to me and said, "Go and speak to him, I'll come with you. If Buck knew you were struggling, and you didn't ask him for help, he would be disappointed. That's what he's here for."

Ann and I approached Buck just as he was sorting out his microphone. He asked me if I was ok and I said, "I'm not a crier, but..." (then I cried a little—slightly mortifying). I told Buck I felt that I was unravelling emotionally, that my horse did not feel connected, and I was unsure what I needed to do/or that if I could do this.

Buck was as calm and serene as usual and said, "Ok, let's see what you've got going on." to which Tuff and I ran through our groundwork. Buck then said, "Well, he looks alright to me. Go and take your time, get him moving out some more and when you're ready, get on." I thanked him, he gave me a smile and said, "You're welcome."

As I walked away, the floodgates opened a bit, and there was a passing of tissues between old and new friends. I set about continuing my groundwork while everyone had mounted up and was listening to Buck, and it was not too long before I joined them. The relief and release I felt was immense. In a short inter-action, Buck had simultaneously taken the immense pressure I'd put on myself from me and redirected me in a positive way. He hadn't given me sympathy or help me wallow and stay in a place of turmoil, he hadn't belittled me or been frustrated at me for being upset; he simply redirected me to where I needed to be mentally, where I could find comfort and relief. It wasn't about my horse; it was an amplified version of what was going on within me, but I think Buck knew that.

Treat them how you want them to be, not how they are. It doesn't just apply to horses.

SWEET MUZZLE

CYNTHIA FUNK

Sweet muzzle of my horse,
velvet skin smelling of grass
whiskers prickling with energy.
Sweet muzzle of my horse,
sacred seat of emotions
dancing with anticipation.
Sweet muzzle of my horse,
nostrils blowing out the primal breath
of a million years of being.
Sweet muzzle of my horse,
raised to the sky in salutation
to the elements and the stars.
Sweet muzzle of my horse,
whispering of wisdom with messages
of taking you too far away places.
Sweet muzzle of my horse.

THE SEED

LINDA DOUGHTY

Dominion
If I don't dominate you,
what will be the definition
of my role in this
relationship?
What is yours?
Are you a guest in my world?
Does buying your hay anoint this small self
as lord and master?
Does my gratitude extend to you
as a plump offering,
a sweet, my servile one?
The way it is
traces
the way it was.

Examination
A test.
Historically speaking
from fetlock to forelock
you have been bought and sold.
I have paid good money, too.

Egalitarianism
Philosophical thought
saunters by, tumbling
into the beyond knowing
of endless night sky.
Star plucked.
We differ.

Sunset
Orange and deep
ephemeral
light
caught
and gone.
This morning your mane is knotted.
Elves?
When tugged the knot remains.
Gently caress the strands,
find the give.
It all falls loose
in beauty.

TWELFTH NIGHT (NOTES FROM JANUARY 6)

KATE BREMER

In this dark week, Olli blows,
Nostrils parting the veil so thin.
Kaya's dreadlocks bundle old
Dreams and nightmares—Wind

Steals ink from a pen; dirt-spun
Roads lead to Mexico, tinsel
Snags on barb wire--donkey
Trails are water and clay for vessels.

17 robins. Ashe juniper creaks
Hello—Earthworms, frogs, and moths
Are out today and us—Freaks
For flying pollen and burro coughs—

Tails switch, burrow down,
'Til February makes a sound.

DREAM HORSE POEMS

LASELL JARETZKI BARTLETT

**Dream Horse
Poem 1**

My Dream Horse.
Best Friend.

Last night I left
your reins untied
and coming to catch you,
you shied,
running but a few steps away,
just beyond my control
yet staying in sight
and inside my heart.

You claim your freedom
unbothered though bound
by bridle and blanket.

(Wild animal or tamed?
When you are your own master
it's never always the same.)

Dream Horse
Poem 2

Oh, Special Horse.
Best Friend.
Dappled Beauty.

Must I leave you in the stable
and ride the white one
who is sure-footed, alert
and bright of eyes,
to climb the highest peak?

Must I leave behind
the delicate one,
the one I have loved to ride,
racing the tides and wind?

Must I forsake you
whose home is my own heart?

Is there no horse fulfilling all my wants?

The highest heights I seek to find,
but the path I do not know.

'Yes' comes the answer.
I must ride the beast
who has made the journey,
whose feet have found the way.

Oh, sadness of ending friendship,
come quickly and be finished with me.

Dream Horse
Poem 3

Beloved Dream Horse.
Divine Surprise!

I ride you again.

Gentle racehorse of great surging power.
To my subtle touch you calm and follow.

Many people gather
and I turn to you
whispering of new discoveries
—modern man's world—
unknown to you
a simple young animal.

Chattering they surround us.
We're oblivious,
attuned to each other
communing
as only best friends and lovers do.

Dream Horse
Poem 4

Dream Horse, is that you?

Wandering through the barn of my childhood
I look up and see
a young shivering
helpless animal
still wet from birth and already
without a mother.

I climb to the loft
to help, to hold.
A snorting ruckus draws me about.
Wild mother coming fierce as a bull.

Two strangers enter:
a drunken woman and farmhand husband.
I see my opportunity to leave and do.

Dream Horse
Poem 5

A young horse.
A tiny baby horse.
An old friend.

Cowering in the corner of my room.

I've come to visit
and among the friends
I forget the hunger of the horse.

Remembering, I go to feed her.

A heavy hard brother mounts her
with tack too much and all askew.
"Get off!" I demand.
He does, and the horse
with a taste of freedom
kicks and romps away.

Slowly I approach and she lets me
catch the reins.
Hello, Friend. You're mine again.

Dream Horse
Poem 6

I lost my horse on the mountain.

I set her free
to roam and graze
and she ran away.
I went home hoping she'd follow
but she didn't.
Is she lost?
Is she freezing
in the unaccustomed deep snows of winter?
Has a hungry mountain lion made a meal of her?

I lost my horse on the mountain.

I am going to search for her
alone
in the middle of the night.
I dress as best I can,
warm against the winter.
The full moon gives me light.
No sleep tonight.
Some things will not wait.

I only need now
a noose
to tie about her neck
to lead her home.
Do you have a length of rope to loan?
I lost my horse on the mountain
and I'm anxious to go.

I hope to find her alive and well,
ready at last
to come home.
I hope I'm lucky and not too late.
I don't think she can live there
with her thin coat and pampered ways.

[Author's note: I wrote these poems over the course of a few months in 1987, directly as I awoke from dreaming. Although largely unedited from the original flow of words, I have adjusted the gender pronouns in the last two poems to reflect my changed relationships with internalized gendered parts. The horse—now female—was initially male.]

PROMENADE

CHRIS KENT

The little dog padded softly along the silent promenade, nose to the ground, sniffing. Overhead, the string of globe lights stretched into the distance, casting an eerie glow around the dog, the walkway, and the lapping waves brushing the shoreline. The fairground rides lurked behind the lights, spookily silent. The ghost train looked ghostly and dark, as one might expect. The brightly painted roller coaster sat, dusty and deserted. It was out of season, which meant the pickings for a little dog were slim. An occasional cold fried potato, maybe a warm coffee cup with sugar stuck to the base, or a hard piece of hot dog. Not many ice cream cones (a particular favourite), or candy floss snippets.

The dog continued padding, intent. As a street dog the search for food was constant. She never knew what she might find, as long as she kept sniffing and searching. She jumped down onto the beach—sometimes the remains of a dead fish may be found. Or, on a really lucky day, a whole crab to be crunched quickly and—head tilted upwards—flipped to the back of the throat and swallowed.

She was a small, neat, black-and-white, appaloosa-spotted dog. She had large black ears, so big they seemed to belong to a different dog. Her bright brown eyes were always alert. She knew how to survive on the streets, scavenging, skulking in the shadows to avoid people and other dogs. She didn't much like the other dogs. Once she had lived with humans and had perfected the skill of stealing a sandwich unnoticed, or cakes from the edge of the table when no one was looking. They did not seem impressed with this skill.

Searching for food was a reassuringly familiar habit that she found hard to stop, even when she wasn't certain she was even hungry. Searching kept her brain occupied, and her brain very much needed to be kept occupied. Sometimes her mind wriggled and squirmed around so much it felt like she would explode. She experienced a constant desire to move and run... or sometimes chew. She used to chew on peoples' clothes, even when they were wearing them. She wondered if that was why the humans closed the door on her and left her on the streets. Or maybe it was the sandwich stealing.

There were always plenty of things to do on the streets, though: places to go, food to find, explorations to make. It was also a little cold and lonely, and she often wished for a warm fire and company. Suddenly she realized she could smell fish. The tide was going out—a good time for investigating the high tide mark—a good place for pickings.

The sun had set in a blaze of golds and greys, all unseen, unnoticed by the little dog. Trotting along the wet sand, her nose working overtime, she suddenly heard a voice far off in the distance. "Izzy! Izzy. Izzy!"

She stopped sniffing to listen.

The voice came again. "Izzy. Izzy. Izzy!" Looking up, she saw the shape of a woman in the distance. With a flash of surprise, she remembered that she was no longer a street dog!

She was Izzy Wizzy. She lived with the human woman. She got fed regularly, had a cosy bed, and other doggy friends whom she rather liked. She often sat on a warm lap, or in front of the glowing wood fire. She went places and did tricks, and played hunting games for toys that smelled interesting, or searched for people. She met lots of people who treated her kindly and children who played good games.

Not a street dog!! How could she have forgotten?

She streaked happily towards her human, slowing only slightly to collect the remains of a slightly mouldy, smashed ice cream cone along the way.

TRUTH SERUM HORSE

TESSA PAGONES

I've been avoiding one of my horses.

If you look at how much I work with my horses (or don't), you'd think I'm avoiding them all, but I'm not. It's true that I can't remember the last time I rode. It's also true that somewhere along the line, riding stopped being the point of having horses for me. Maybe it never was.

One of my favorite horse books when I was a kid was The Secret Horse. It was about two girls who stole a horse who was about to be euthanized from an animal shelter in the middle of Washington D.C. They hid him away on a not-quite abandoned property, without the knowledge of or permission from either their families or the caretakers of the property. I grew up in D.C., and in my mind, I still know the exact houses in my neighborhood I pictured them living in, and I know the property, a whole city block square in my memory, where they kept the horse. They groomed the horse a lot, and fed him loads of cut grass they carried to the barn on sheets after it dried to hay in the sun, and at one point they took turns getting on him bareback with a halter and walking slowly around the barnyard. Despite the many, many books I read about girls winning unexpected ribbons at horse shows, The Secret Horse always stood out as my kind of horse story.

I had my own secret horse eventually, though I bought her

instead of stealing her, and I kept her at barns where the barn owners knew she was there. She was, however, a secret from my parents.

I bought her from a farm where I worked before I left for college, and then had her transported several states away to join me in Vermont. I kept her for three of the four years I was there, working odd jobs to pay her board, and borrowing cars and bicycles so I could get to the barn to see her. I eventually sold her, all without ever telling my parents I had owned a horse.

As things often turn out in my family, the real secret was that my mother knew about my secret horse almost the whole time. The barn I bought her from had called my parents' house at some point after I left for college and before I had her trailered up to join me, and my mother had answered the phone. I don't know what conversation took place, because it was one more thing we never discussed. The horse's name, it may be relevant to note, was Stretch the Truth.

The horse I have been avoiding has a name, but we often refer to him as the Truth Serum Horse.

He earned this nickname when I had him for sale once, for five or ten minutes. It was one of those times I didn't feel like I was doing enough with him, and that maybe he should be in a barn where someone would ride him more. I ran an ad that more or less said "I have a big brown horse that I don't want to sell. Call me if you have to." One person must have been intrigued enough by the ambiguity of the ad to call. She came to see him, her best friend and husband in tow.

I rode him first, and he started out really rough and feeling like he was about to blow—a not insignificant event in a horse as big and athletic as he is. I was on his back feeling like "Here I am calling myself a horse trainer and he looks like he doesn't know the very basic basics and I look like I can't ride a carousel horse." I stopped and looked at these three strangers and said "I just quit one of my jobs today and it's a job I thought I always wanted but it turned out to be terrible and now I've quit it and

I'm relieved and sad at the same time and my brain is really distracted." Then I took a breath, picked up the reins, and the horse moved off like an old schoolmaster and went beautifully through his paces.

The woman who was interested in buying him got on next and started off similarly, the horse looking tense and awkward, and the rider looking grim and miserable. Suddenly she said "I hate riding in front of people, even people I know—I'm so nervous that they think I'm incompetent and doing everything wrong that I don't even remember to breathe." Just as suddenly she and the horse clicked into a smooth, soft jog trot and she spent the rest of her ride grinning from ear to ear.

Her friend and her husband rode the horse with almost identical patterns, the rough rides smoothing out as soon as they blurted out what was bothering them. I have no doubt that the horse made that happen—he needed everyone to get over how they were trying to look, and to just be how they actually were.

Horses have varied tolerance for people whose insides and outsides don't match. Some horses just tune it out. One horse I had would see me coming when I was in a certain mood and turn and walk away. "Nope. You are not getting on me today. Not with that attitude." The Truth Serum Horse doesn't have a low tolerance, he has zero tolerance for being around people whose insides and outsides are out of integrity. I could insist, but only by shutting him down entirely, and I got out of the forcing-horses-into-a-mental-shutdown business years ago.

The Truth Serum Horse came to me with numerous issues from how he was trained in his first few years. While I have helped him to feel better physically, and about life in general, I have not really helped him to get past his problem areas. I mostly just avoid them, and if I don't feel like that is working, I avoid him. It has only very recently come to my attention that this is pretty close to my own path of making some progress toward the way I say I want to be, but then avoiding meaningful, lasting change. No wonder I want to avoid the horse who insists that I not only look at the underlying thing but admit it. Out loud.

Because I think of myself as a horse trainer with a specialty in "fixing" troubled horses, I tend to look at horses in terms of how I can help them be more comfortable with the things I want them to do. The Truth Serum Horse has made it clear he won't be comfortable unless I become more comfortable with the things he wants me to do. It's taken me a lot of years, and a horse who won't accept anything less than the truth, to realize that the one I need to fix is me.

FIELD OF FOALS

CYNTHIA FUNK

Field of foals,
lying on a carpet of emeralds,
Mother Earth feeding them.
Field of foals,
basking in the warmth of the Texas sunshine,
dreaming of play with their unicorn friends.
Field of foals,
mother mare guarding over her precious one,
so proud of creating this life.
Field of foals,
growing up to be the love of some young girl's dreams,
precious being of God's love.
Field of foals,
frolicking, your fresh new energy brings tears of joy to my eyes,
I am blessing you all on this beautiful planet we call New Earth.
Field of foals.

CONNECTION

AMANDA JANE LARAMORE

The mountains of Crested Butte beckon us. Part of the ritual of restoring balance and recharging is getting away in nature. The fall foliage is breathtaking. The leaves of the aspen trees offer brilliant shades of gold, amber, and crimson that shimmer under bluebird skies. Phil and I are hand in hand. We look at each other and smile. We are going for a trail ride on horseback.

Phil knows I only have eyes for my favorite horse Ghost. At this point in a four-year tradition, we are old friends. Ghost and I share a kinship and affinity for one another. He stands sixteen and a half hands, lean, a white Missouri Foxtrotter with soft dark eyes and a mane of flowing white silk, reminiscent of angel's wings.

We traverse the mountain terrain as one. I trust Ghost carrying me as we make our way uphill. He bears the weight of my physical body and he carries all of my burdens. He meets me where I am. Filled with gratitude and warmth despite the cool autumn air, I am in awe sharing this experience with him.

The connection we share as I ride on his back is meditative. Ghost and I see through the same eyes, the ever-changing scenery and marvel at the landscape. Nature now offers us the promise of transformation as we gain elevation. The aspen trees are replaced with blue spruce and ponderosa pine. The air becomes colder and we catch scents of citrus and dirt.

I watch Ghost's ears constantly moving, alert and attuned to things far beyond the capability of my senses. I look at Ghost and feel pride and contentment. I want time to be still and savor this picturesque heartfelt moment before we must part. I do not want to leave Ghost. I feel a lump in my throat. I scan the silvery body I have memorized and know it like a lover.

The next trip to the mountains, Ghost is still waiting for me. Another crisp, fall day, my senses are invigorated, and my heart is full. Then the owner, Chuck mentions that he is retiring Ghost saying that his hocks are sore, the trails are too steep, and the rides are too long. My heart pounds in my chest, I feel light-headed. I have imagined this moment for years. I have made several of the more significant and serious decisions in my life impulsively. Intuitiveness and love are my guides, I go with it. Ghost moves to a barn five minutes from our home.

Ghost becomes my Ghostie, easily adjusting to retirement. His job now is to be loved and know that he is in his forever home. We visit him four times a day. Phil falls in love with him, and that part of Phil's soul is awakened. The adoration and love are mutual. We feel our duty to honor Ghost's service. For more than 8 years, Ghost carried hundreds of people from all over the world on trail rides. Ghost was a dedicated and obedient servant to these people. Now it is our turn to be his servant.

In the months since Ghost has come to live with us, he speaks to me in almost literal ways. After a year of being with us, I notice a change in Ghost. He speaks to me and I write a text message to myself so I will remember. Sometimes these Ghostie messages come in the middle of the night. Other times when we are together. They all are a version of "I am hurting and tired."

Our veterinarian recommends x rays and a lameness test. There is a specialist and new language full of numbers like "four out of five" describing severe pain. We find the only remaining option for his cartilage-less joints vowing that we will do anything to provide physical comfort to our dear Ghostie.

The first injection is on a September morning and, even on that first day of hope a friend from the barn calls to say that Ghost will not get up. We have repeated days when he cannot get up. He has a colic episode. After weeks, the medication finally takes full effect. Still, Ghost's hock drags at times. We witness him fall in the mud while playing with his best bud, Sundancer. He struggles to get up. At lunchtime one day, I note that he is sweating profusely standing at the gate. I lay my hand against his body where a girth no longer goes and feel that his heart rate is elevated. The veterinarian can only attribute it to pain. The medication we were so hopeful would support and offer comfort and pain management is not successful. Ghost's messages keep coming to me.

A winter storm leaves the ground blanketed in more than a foot of snowfall. Ghost is wearing his blue winter blanket. He's dragging his leg and moving slowly. I give him Bute daily to ease the pain. The two months of medical treatment do not support his ailing body.

I cannot ignore the messages I am receiving from Ghost any longer. Selfishly I do not want to believe what I am hearing. We confer with our vet, friends, and an animal communicator. The enormity of this decision, the one I cannot even name because it breaks my heart, is painstaking and an awesome responsibility. There is no right or wrong here. I put my trust in our connection and relationship.

Phil and I sit at the kitchen counter listening intently to what Ghost has to say. The message is clear and received. In our hearts we know what has to be done. He's asked us for help crossing over. Our hearts are breaking, but we will honor his wish.

"Help me to cross over. My body is nearing its end. I want you to help me to get to that space where I can leave my physical body. I want you to see how my body is failing me. I have only been appreciated for my body until now. I am with my heart family. I am honored to be a part of this family. Now my spirit and soul are recognized. I have never experienced so much love.

Pay attention and know that I am guiding you to the right time and place and it will be perfect. There is spiritual rebirth and more to come, I will be a guardian angel to you and Phil. I will stay with you talk with you and be right there. I feel your love all of the time. Our connection was made for this."

We make the excruciating decision. With deep listening we observe Ghost's request.

Approaching December 7th, 2019, Phil and I cry as we walk together, we cry as we eat together, we cry as we drive together, we cry ourselves to sleep, we cry alone. The lessons I carry with me become a recitation and mantra. We are born on a breath; we die on a breath. Death ends a life, not a relationship.

After C.S. Lewis's wife passed, he eloquently said, "No one ever told me that grief felt so much like fear." The dread and pain I feel in my chest burns, as a physical ache. I am drenched in fear.

Phil observes the moon in its cycle. Can we stop the moon in its cycle to have more time with our beloved horse? We spend time loving and loving and loving him.

Our ritual and blessing to you,
it is a good day to die our friend.

Our tears flow like a river, you will never know thirst,

Our longing for you yields endless
green pasture and mountains to roam.

Our love for you births wings.

Soar with the Great Spirit my Soul-Shine.

Dance in the stars until we meet again.

I will be a friend like you.

I will forgive like you.

I will be grounded like you.

I will breathe like you.

I will connect like you.

I will know like you.

I will seek harmony like you.

I will love like you.

I will be all of these things to honor you.

The night before Ghost took flight, we were feeding him and Sundancer. My eyes lifted to the sky to witness a bald eagle flying over us. I don't see it as a coincidence. Phil and I weep at the beauty and significance of this message from the universe.

On the breath of dawn, I awake to the sound of an owl near our home. Phil hears it too.

The vet arrives. The symbolism of his last walk over the bridge is etched in my mind. My eyes sting watching Phil and Ghostie together, moving farther and farther from me. Sundancer now stands alone in the paddock with me. I exhale and walk to join Phil and Ghost at the back of the barn where we have chosen for him to lay his tired body down.

We play The Allman Brothers song "Soul-Shine," Widespread Panic's "Travelin' Light" and Willie Nelson's song "Ride me Back Home," the lyrics represent Ghost and our ode to his tender-hearted spirit. We light sage and frankincense to support his soul's ascension.

Our friend Jen came to be with us and hold ceremony over Ghost's body. She took a photograph of his eye and I ask why. As a Hospice nurse of decades, she shares that she has only experienced this once with a child who had died. The child's soul had not left their body. Jen shares that "he is still here with you." After several hours of blessing Ghost's body and mourning, we say our final adieu. He lies on the ground adored in red rose petals and sunflowers. Jen stays with him. Later that day she shared that when we walked away, she felt Ghost accompany us as he left his physical body.

Days later I feel a profound peace. Ghost breathes into me, integrated. I feel the wisdom, love, grace, and courage Ghost embodied enter into me. Ghost is buried at Evergreen cemetery among old equine friends and a herd of bison. White bison adorn the landscape at this sacred burial ground.

Hours after Ghost had been taken to his final resting place, I walk around his pen crying and asking for a sign. I am enveloped in emptiness, yet my eyes are drawn to the left of the creek. An egret stands still. We gaze at each other.

The egret represents the connection between this world and the Spirit world.

I feel Ghost with me. I hear him communicate with me. We have so much more to do together, in spite of our physical separation. The egret regularly presents himself to us in flight at dusk. We watch him until he is out of sight. We exhale. All is well with my soul; peace is present despite Ghost's physical absence.

As I look at Ghost's horseshoes that have been molded into hearts hanging as a wind chime in Phil's office, I hear the metal touch and the sound reverberates with Ghost's light and eternal presence.

A few months later, I see the egret soaring above the treetops. I hear Ghost: *I am always with you. I am giving you strength. You kept your word my soul friend. Our connection continues.*

THAT HUGE ENGINE

ABBY LETTERI

"We just stood there
In stunned silence.
We couldn't believe it.
The heart was perfect." *

Before there was Secretariat, there was the 60s.
I pressed my awkward girl body to the speaker,
To the unholy events that marked us.
10,000 planes shot down and my mother's bare lips
Pressed together in grief.
The world shed that decade as I shed my girl skin,
Took refuge in a dusty barn where Jose and Luis
Carried water and photos of their babies
In Mexico. Talk of the big chestnut
On everyone's lips.
We worked hard that day and left early,
The one and only time we ever did.
Raced home to watch the big chestnut
Moving like a tremendous machine, 31 lengths ahead,
Jockey looking over his shoulder in disbelief.
Jose and Luis in the tack room with a transistor
Seeing as a blind man sees baseball, vivid,
The big chestnut a fiery comet of sinew, muscle, and bone.

Us in the living room, stunned and breathless.
That huge engine powering us all home.

*Dr Thomas Swerczek, head Pathologist at the University of Kentucky, while performing a necropsy on Secretariat.

RIDING THROUGH

ELAINE KIRSCH EDSALL

We all arrive at fear with real and imaginary experiences that are as unique to us as our DNA.

Unlike any other marathon, fear has no common starting place, no midway motivation point and no perceivable end, but if we can gain succour from refreshments offered along the way, we can survive. If we can hear the shouts of encouragement through the deafening cacophony of self-doubt, we have hope, and if we can accept that our personal best is simply putting one foot in front of the other, we'll stay the distance. The absence of a finishing line will become irrelevant.

What are your greatest fears? Mine are incapacitating illness, living without my husband, and I'm fearful when riding my horse. I have not listed them in order of greatness.

Life without Mark is self-explanatory. Being incapacitated means I don't want to helplessly linger on the edge of death; I want to say a quick "Goodbye," grab my coat, and leave while you still have something bad to say about me.

My most closely guarded secret is that I'm a fearful rider. I could never say riding frightens me, so is there a difference between feeling fearful and feeling frightened, and where do these feelings originate?

I love my horse with all my heart. I love riding, and the joy it brings is like nothing else in the world. Yet, every time I climb into the saddle, all pleasure is obliterated by the voice of fear screaming relentlessly in my head. It tells me I have just signed my own death warrant. Like a spit roast over an open fire, my fear rotates continually, basted by terror and dread. The juices are so intensely flavoured I can taste them dripping down the back of my throat.

So, what do we do with fear? I can't predict what fate has in store for Mark, any more than I can arrange my demise as a speedy episode between breakfast and lunch. But surely there is a way to restore the equilibrium of riding my horse?

The fear has been with me for many years; I just chose to ignore it. Ignorance was bliss but it wasn't constructive. Mind and muscle memories have replayed past events so many times in a vain effort to warn me of the peril, that what started as a faint speck of anxiety has become an overwhelming stain of panic.

When I mount my horse, I breathe deeply and focus mindfully on my actions. I smile as my body lightly greets the saddle, and sigh like granny settling into her favourite chair. I thank my horse, check my girth, wriggle my toes, shrug my shoulders and thank my horse again. All is good.

Lightly and politely, I ask my horse to move off. Bruce responds (as always) with a quick snatch of the reins, and a wobbly hind step as his dodgy hip adjusts to my weight. We both breathe through his momentary anxiety, and I thank him again for his compliance, and for being him. We walk down the track to the arena, his steps are guarded as unshod hooves tread on stones, and he re-sets his balance to negotiate downhill with a slanting camber. We've done this hundreds of times, and don't deviate from his favoured route, arriving at the arena in the correct place to open the gate, enter and shut it behind us with well-executed sidesteps and turns.

We begin our swinging, relaxed walk up the long side of the school towards the top, and as Bruce pricks his ears and raises his head to better see the horse grazing beyond, I feel my hands tighten, my face reddens. I have a lucid moment of trying to regain composure before the panic in my gut rises to meet the panic descending from my eyeballs. I start to sing aloud, and Bruce's ears flick back to me, as the familiar words of 'Ten Green Bottles' follow him around the school perimeter. He walks mechanically forward as if I wasn't there (which I'm not), and I try to let his solid body soothe me. My panic swirls around, before joining forces with a heartbeat that's faster than speeding time. It's a gamble whether I'll implode or explode, and I grit my teeth awaiting the outcome.

"Breathe...breathe...green bottles..." I gasp "hanging on the wall..." gasp "if breathe breathe green bottles..." gasp "should accidentally fall..." two gasps and an outbreath "and there'll be nine green bottles" outbreath "hanging on the frigging wall."

Throughout all this, I smile and pretend. My stoic horse rubs his nose on his knee and pretends; the critical fault-pickers who watch surreptitiously would never know how much each ride costs. When I've put myself through enough penury to prove we're both 'ticking over nicely,' we halt squarely to dismount, and as my leaden legs reach terra firma, the frustration of my feeble fear kills me slowly once again. I can't even manage a walk around the arena. It's been a year since we ventured out of the farm on horseback, and two years since we trotted. Once I'm standing on the ground, Bruce shakes himself from head to toe, ridding his body of my burden, and rests his nose on my shoulder; he knows a placatory peppermint will follow the litany of apologies.

Where did this fear begin? In the beginning is the only answer. Countless horses over countless years have done things that scared me, but I always coped with whatever they did. Bruce added his substantial weight to the fear load; from the start, he had an unpredictable streak belied by his steadfast appearance, and when he accelerated from fright to flight quicker than I could anticipate, it took a chunk of courage to sit still.

When I recall the events without emotion, I clearly see I

coped competently, if not entirely effectively, but fearful feelings cloud logic. I'm not frightened of the horse; I've managed the worst he might do. What frightens me is the feeling of fear.

My confidence waxes and wanes with the stages of my cancer treatments, but I recognize the real Me differs from the chemotherapy-induced wraith, who wouldn't dare put foot in a stirrup. I no longer have anything to prove, least of all to myself and in a skewed way, fear reminds me I'm still alive. Perhaps it's time to accept that fear is as much a part of riding as limbs aching the next day? My fear is mine, and I'm grateful for the reminder not to do something dangerous, but like an auto-immune condition, fear doesn't know how to stop. So, is the answer to work on its responsiveness and not its potency? A stronger bit is never the answer for a horse, so perhaps walk-halt-walk transitions with my fear would work, direction not correction?

Being a competent partner for Bruce began when I learnt to sit still, breathe and trust, instead of trying to control with dominance, which was as simple as it was difficult. Could fear be diluted by guiding it to a place of acceptance, rather than obliteration?

I am a consummate saleswoman, it's what I do. I sell things for a living and I've managed to sell myself to myself all these years in a convincing game of smoke and mirrors, so could I also sell myself a life without fear? It was a challenge I could not resist.

Like all horses, Bruce has a strict moral code that does not trust sales pitches. He shut the door in my face each time I presented myself with a re-invented mask and new set of false dialogue; he knew it was still the same me. Eventually he stopped bothering to answer the door and pinned a notice on the front window that read 'come back when you tell the truth'. That horse speaks his mind; he is no schmoozer. In the end, the only resource left was to strike a deal and agree we would both tell the truth.

Bruce is a stoic horse and he'd chosen to shut down rather

than dump the burden he carried, so it wasn't easy for him either.

My side of the bargain was that if I didn't understand something I'd say so, stop pretending, and allow us to work together. I promised I would become my authentic self so that what he saw was what he got, although I had no idea who or what that was. He made no such promises because horses aren't that needy, but basically, we were both going to cut the crap, and I would always listen if he wanted to say something. Living with a horse is like living with a four-legged lie detector, and Bruce was definitely going to tell me if fearlessness became another pretence.

Ten years ago, when I first had Bruce, I found myself adrift in a minefield of fear and broken dreams. I'd expected my rescue horse to relax and rejoice in his liberation, but misplaced adoration was no substitute for structure. As he took the necessary steps to safeguard himself at all costs, he grew more anxious and bullish and I grew more scared. We were both in a situation we couldn't handle, and in a misguided struggle to regain the upper hand, I thought false bravado would give me power. It didn't, but it began the journey towards giving me something much better. Understanding.

As all good horses are wont to do, Bruce led me towards different teaching methods and better insight. How horses do this is one of the great unsolved mysteries of all time. After meeting Kirsty, who taught differently to anyone I knew and introduced me to a new way of working, Bruce deposited me at Anna's Relaxed & Forward barn in a cloud of dust. My debt to this horse is infinite for facilitating my momentous personality overhaul.

A random comment 'Did you know your fear is afraid as well? Your fear is afraid to stop trying to protect you' really struck a chord with me, because I was a born people pleaser, my job was to make things better. By fighting my fear, I'd inadvertently upset it and made things worse. Now the dynamic had changed I could be the prime motivator, making amends by helping my fear protect me, because as we all know, it is easier to help someone else than to help yourself.

I renamed fear Early Warning System, hoping this would dilute the connotations fear evoked; a positive name for something facilitating a safer life and not an inhibited one. I felt my fear didn't get more anxious as I got more confident, because it wanted me confident. It wanted to take a backseat and only went into overdrive when it felt unheeded. My Early Warning System simply wanted to protect me, and then it wanted to sit with its feet up and enjoy doing nothing.

Fear is just a feeling, the same as happiness and sorrow, it is part of us, and I think we need to celebrate that fact. Selling myself a life without fear isn't the answer, but I would like to live alongside what I now understand is an ally. I am not pretending (to you or myself) that I've suddenly become brave or confident. I'm not telling my horse I can do this, because he knows what I can and I can't do before that information reaches my own brain.

There are no set plans for how to deal with fear; it's a suck-it-and-see situation because what works one day may not work the next. Everything in life changes; right now, this is how fear presents itself, this is where I am, and it feels exactly the right place. If an Early Warning System also allows other things to come to the forefront, things that I may never have considered when galloping across country, then that's a fair compromise.

Mindfulness teaches us not to hang on to feelings good or bad. All we have to do is acknowledge them and let them pass. Something so simple should be easy but we all know it is not. I think working on letting fear go, and not trying to quell it with dominance is the way forward, however difficult that might be.

This morning I talked it over with my horse. He was busy doing the important stuff of eating spring grass and scratching his nose, so he didn't say much while I spoke. As I finished my explanation, he lifted his head, flicked his tail and studied me for a good few seconds, with ears pricked forward. Then he went back to eating. I consider that a yes, because this time, the door stayed open.

Today I've shared my secret, aired my fear, and I feel lighter. Life is a work in progress, and perhaps by keeping our enemies closer than our friends, we can choose when we visit them, instead of having them hammer on our door demanding entry.

My horse, my ride, my fear. My choice.

ANIMALS ARE LUCKY

TESSA PAGONES

I killed my first chicken
fresh out of the egg,
its insides

mostly on the outside.
I took its soft weightlessness
from the heat

of the incubator.
Found the back of its neck
with my thumb,

and pressed
against the edge of a table.
I felt the tiny

vertebrae part
and the spinal cord snap.
I cupped the

warm body
in my hands, while it twitched
and flopped, and lay still.

      I killed my first sheep

in the hallway of the lab,
held still,

sitting up,
head bent to one side.
I pressed the

jugular vein
or something near enough to it
and hoped for an

obvious place
to insert the needle.
I aimed and stuck,

pulled back,
blood welling into the syringe.
Pushed sedative, then green

potassium chloride.
After, I listened with a stethoscope
to hear the heart

not beat,
but mostly watching its eyes,
waiting for the life to go out.

> I killed my last pig
> with the same bright green solution.
> She was already
>
> sedated, unconscious,
> infection spread through her jaw,
> and yet I hesitated,
>
> looking down at her ear.
> The web of veins and arteries

branched through

the pink skin -
the same pattern mirrored
in the skin of

my wrist.
I held the syringe, weighed the choice.
Where to insert the needle?

Animals are lucky
My mother often said
In the years between

When the cancer came back
And when it killed her.
Animals are lucky

that people can choose for them
the time and manner
of their death.

I wonder which death
she would prefer
at whose hands,

and when she died
in the hospice bed,
if she chose

or I did.

THE ROOSTER SANCTUARY

BY SUSAN KETCHEN

Madeline has apparently believed Google Maps' driving estimate instead of mine and is an hour late for our two o'clock appointment when she arrives outside my office door. I don't take it personally. After all, I have lied to her, though not about this.

I watch Madeline through my office window. Okay, it's not really an office, it's a feed room, but I have a filing cabinet in one corner and a sign on the door that says "Office" to encourage customers to stop here and not drive the rest of the way up to the house where the other facilities are.

Madeline is sitting in her SUV, blotting under her eyes with a tissue, being careful to not smudge her mascara. She's been crying. Most of them do.

After a moment, she exits her car and pops the hatch. I stroll out to meet her by the picnic table. She has the cardboard box gripped close against her body, fingers slipped inside the vent holes slashed at the corners. I can tell she's not ready to let him go, so I breathe slowly and give her some time.

"You're Jill?" she asks, and when I nod, she says, "I'm Madeline."

"Yes, I thought so." It would be unkind to add anything about her being late.

She completely skips the small talk, which frankly is a great relief to me. "I've had him since he was born," she says. "I carried him from the incubator in the palm of my hand. Not that I knew he was a he."

"I know. It's very difficult. I wish there was something I could say to make it easier."

"I told him he'd have a forever home with me, and now look at what I'm doing."

"What you're doing is a kindness. Others might have used him for soup."

Madeline considers my comment with obvious horror, her eyes brimming with tears. "I could . . . I could never . . . eat . . . .."

As much as I try not to, I almost always manage to say something that upsets people. They are all fragile; the tough ones choose another option and don't end up at my door.

Madeline lowers the box to the ground but rests a foot across the folded top flaps. I prepare myself for a longer afternoon. Some need the therapy session while others just use the drop-off box at the bottom of the hill.

"He makes a lot of noise. His crowing wakes me, and I can't get back to sleep. My health is suffering." She coughs; I know she's just emphasizing her point, but I take a reflexive step back anyway, and six feet increases to nine.

"It's really not my place to judge," I say.

"I should never have hatched chickens at all. But I thought that with the pandemic we should be more self-sufficient. Obviously, I'm not cut out to be a farmer."

"Oh, I wouldn't say that. I had a good business even before the pandemic. Surplus roosters have been a problem for a long time."

I watch Madeline survey my facility. There are thirty roosters milling about in the paddock beside my office and another forty-five across the creek. It's an absolute glory of iridescent plumage, but Madeline sees only the infrastructure. "That's good fencing," she says. "What is it—eight feet high? And is that an electric wire along the top?"

"It discourages the bears." Since she's already having trouble sleeping, I don't mention the raptors, owls, mink, or raccoons, all of whom have a fondness for chicken.

The rooster in the box flaps his wings and starts to crow. Within seconds, his challenge is met by every rooster on the property.

"Jesus," says Madeline. "How do you stand it?"

I shrug. "Every time I hear a rooster crow, I'm reminded that I've prolonged a life and solved a problem for a kind-hearted person like you."

She squints at me suspiciously, looking I suppose for signs of irony. I give her a little smile.

"You're lucky you don't have neighbours," says Madeline. "Your driveway must be five miles long. I'd never have found you without that Google Maps pin."

She takes a folded paper from her pocket and flattens it on the picnic table then steps away so I can move close enough to read. It's the application form from my Rooster Sanctuary Facebook page, all the blanks now filled with tidy blue handwriting.

"You don't get scared out here in the middle of nowhere?" asks Madeline while I read. "Not scared," I say without looking up. Lonely sometimes, but there are worse things. Phillip had been very difficult until he was ready to leave; he'd made lonely seem tantalizing. I point to a line on the form. "You want the Short Stay package," I say evenly, trying not to trigger her defensiveness, but out of the corner of my eye I can see she has folded her arms anyway.

"Well, one month is how long in chicken time: about a year?" She shakes her head. "I can't believe I'm paying board for a rooster. It's seventy-five dollars out of our grocery money for heaven's sake, and my husband hasn't worked since the shutdown."

I won't argue, but in my opinion, seventy-five dollars is a small price to pay to assuage a guilty conscience. She could spend that much or more for a therapist in town or sleeping prescriptions.

"I'll need to attach a leg band before we let him out of the box. That's how I keep track— every bird is color coded." I pull a handful of zip ties from my pocket and select a yellow one from the rainbow of options. "Yellow means September," I say. "Your fella will be able to enjoy what's left of July and the entire month of August."

Madeline is peering at the roosters closest to us, searching for zip ties. "I feel so guilty. What do most people buy?"

"One month, just like you." I'd designed the options carefully. Boarding was twenty-five dollars per month with a one-month minimum because I didn't want it to look like I was running a straight abattoir. On top of that was the fifty dollar "processing" fee to cover disposal when boarding was finished. "Though there are a few birds here for a year. And there's one out there with a black leg band, and he's here for life."

"A thousand bucks? Who can afford that?"

I'm drawing breath to remind her that my services are confidential when she waves her hands back and forth, erasing the air. "Oh, I don't really want to know, I was being rhetorical." She opens her wallet and slides out the money. It's always cash. I make it clear on my Facebook page that I prefer e-transfer, but I guess no one wants the transaction to be traceable, as if what we're doing is illegal or immoral. I remind myself that I am a good person, doing a good thing. Even the lying is for a good purpose.

Still she hesitates. "How do I know you'll let him live the whole month? What's to stop you from doing him in tonight?"

"We have a contract, and I stand by every word." It's easier to lie now that she's questioned my integrity. "Just imagine him here, chasing bugs and having a good time."

She extends her arm and the bills quiver at the tip of her fingers. I point to the bucket beside my office door, and she drops them in.

"Where'd you get this idea anyway?" she asks, not warmly.

"Doesn't it ever seem like you're taking advantage of people in pain?"

I understand that folks who are suffering can say hurtful things. I calmly explain to her that I'd seen countless posts on Facebook from people trying to give away roosters. "Obviously there was a need, and a secret world of dissatisfaction, guilt—"

"At least I'm not the only one," Madeline interrupts.

"Of course not. People make mistakes, they paint themselves into corners. Most folks don't like killing things. They just need an option."

"But a seventy-five dollar minimum? Don't you think you're profiting off the pandemic?"

"I have costs. Feed, fencing, humane euthanasia equipment. And I don't enjoy killing any more than you do. I provide a service. I think it's worth something."

Madeline considers this while I open the box, grab the rooster, attach the zip tie, then drop him in the segregation pen. I wish she'd leave, but she stands there, her fingers hooked through the page wire, and stares at her bird.

"He's actually pretty handsome," she says wistfully. "I was so busy hating and resenting him, I forgot how good looking he was."

"There's not much point hating something for behaving according to its nature," I say. "It's not as though he was trying to wake you up every night." Which obviously was a mistake.

She had turned towards her car but then stopped. "You know, I don't think you should call your place a sanctuary. It's false advertising. Sanctuaries are supposed to keep animals safe for the rest of their lives."

"All you have to do is pay me."

"No way, not for this. You know what places are called that collect the unwanted? Concentration camps. But that wouldn't be such a good business on Facebook, would it?"

And with that, she leaves.

I watch her car disappearing down the driveway, returning

her to a better life, problem solved. She can tell her friends she found a home for her rooster. She won't call it a concentration camp because that would reflect poorly on her. She'll call it a sanctuary. And it is—because I lied. I lie every time; I lie in person and I lie on Facebook. Because I don't kill the roosters at the end of one month or six or twelve. I love the glorious noisy unwanted bastards. Sure, some of them die, I can't keep the predators out all the time. And sometimes there's too much competitive aggression and one rooster is killed by another, or mortally wounded and I have to humanely euthanize.

I could never advertise this though. I'd look like a crazy cat lady and people would be throwing their surplus roosters over my fence or leaving them on my driveway. I'd be overrun, with zero income.

It's true that, financially, the pandemic has been good to me. I'm a fortunate person to be able to make a positive contribution by staying home, removing burdens of shame and inadequacy from my customers. It's a service I'm proud of, and in its small way, it is satisfying.

The sun is going down and I'm closing the office door when I hear a vehicle approaching on the gravel road. It stops out of sight at the bottom of the hill. I hear women's voices through the trees, and the clang of a tailgate dropping open. I decide to give them a bit of time. For some people the shame is too deep. And they always pay, there will be money in an envelope; no one has ever stiffed me. So, I give them some space and privacy.

I hear two doors close, the engine revs, and tires bite into the gravel.

I wander down the driveway and see the box as I round the corner. It is larger than the ones people usually drop off. As I draw closer, I see the envelope taped to the side, a brown business-sized one, and it is bulging.

The box sways from side to side. The flaps are secured with duct tape. There is one vent hole, larger than I would have recommended for a chicken, and as I watch, a limb thrusts through it. I step closer. It is a man's arm. On the wrist is a single black zip tie.

This shouldn't be too difficult. Phillip had arrived with three.

*There's power in allowing
yourself to be known and heard.
In owning your unique story,
in using your authentic voice.*

Michelle Obama

MEET THE AUTHORS

Eve Allen

I am a freelance writer and editor. I started writing creatively at age 12. I write fiction, including short stories, a novel, a play, and a television script. I also write essays. My work has been featured on my website, literary magazines, multiple websites, and as part of *What She Wrote*, an anthology book of women writers. Find more of my work here:

https://riverwritereve.wordpress.com/

Lori Araki

Lori Araki is an equine therapeutic riding instructor, certified through PATH, International. She has studied riding with Olympic medalists in dressage and three-day eventing. Her goals include teaching kindness and compassion along with heels down and eyes up, being a better ukulele player, and seeing the northern lights from horseback in Iceland.

Nicole Artz

Nicole has always enjoyed writing as a way of making sense of the world. Her first book, "Geraldine" celebrated the life of the beloved class guinea pig that helped her survive third grade. Although never published it was carefully illustrated and laminated by hand. Nicole went on to become a physician and currently practices palliative care in Des Moines, Iowa. She is certified in equine facilitated learning and enjoys partnering with horses to help medical students and resident physicians learn skills to support personal growth and well-being. She has continued to write and publishes short blogs at

www.MonarchEquine.org

Sarah Virginia Barnes

When Sarah is not writing historical fiction, along with the occasional poem, she teaches riding as a meditative art. She holds a Ph.D. in history from Northwestern University and spent many years as a college professor before turning full-time to riding and writing. Sarah and her husband have two grown daughters and live in the foothills outside Boulder, CO with their dogs. Although Sarah's husband is extremely tolerant of her equine obsession, he is also severely allergic, so Sarah's horses live nearby rather than at home. She is currently finishing her first novel, *She Who Rides Horses*. Contact Sarah at:

sarah@anamcaraequestrian.com

Lasell Jaretzki Bartlett

Lasell Jaretzki Bartlett expresses her pioneer spirit through writing and in person - as horsewoman, educator, and somatic therapist - helping people navigate the internalized landscapes of their relationships with themselves and other beings. As a near-death survivor, Lasell embraces grief and resilience, seeking to make meaning of life and bring light to dying.

She lives with her beloved and a variety of animal friends in rural Virginia where she enjoys equine, writing, and gardening activities. Her writings have been published in *The Natural Horse Magazine* and in Mark Rashid's *A Journey To Softness*. You can find Lasell at:

http://lasellbartlett.wordpress.com
and www.lasellbartlett.com

Patti Brehler

Patti Brehler is young-at-heart enough to bicycle 3800 miles solo, crazy enough to write a book about it, and old enough that her adventure-travel memoir is a "coming of a certain age" reflection of her life lived as art. Her stories illustrate how calculated risks foster extraordinary synchronicity within her universe.

Now retired from freelancing for a small Michigan newspaper, patti has been a record-setting ultra-marathon bicyclist, journeyman machinist, massage therapist, adventure coach, bicycle store owner, dog trainer, and amateur death doula for her parents.

Somewhere in there was a short stint as a railroad conductor. pattibrehler@gmail.com

Kate Bremer

Kate Bremer lives in the rocky hill country of Central Texas with cats, dogs, burros and a horse. She loves to host writing and drumming circles with the beautiful herd to offer people an experience of nature, creativity, and fellowship. Her website is:

www.foresthorse.com

Wendi A. Clouse

Wendi A. Clouse creates poetry that explicates the emotional and too often concealed realities of women. With a Ph.D. from the University of Colorado, Wendi often uses the intersection between poetry and anthropological theory to pull back the veil on tensions created from the interaction of the constructed self and social expectation. In the past few years, she has had several works published by The Whisper and the Roar, A Feminist Literary Collective, and Tiny Flames Press. Wendi is completing work for her first chapbook, *The Music of Whispering Horses*

and Other Lies, which she plans to present in late 2021.
stateofcake@hotmail.com

Joanna Savage Coleman

Jo is a queer poet and artist living in Wiradjuri country, Australia. She performs competitive spoken-word and wears a size EU39 shoe. She lives with a rabbit, a dog, and constant feelings of existential dread.
www.joannasavagecoleman.com

Linda Doughty

Linda Doughty came out as a writer in the barn. She is now retired from her professional career as a classical flute player and has reclaimed her childhood passions for horses and writing. She lives in Tucson, Arizona.
https://horsebackwritingflute.home.blog/

Elaine Kirsch Edsall

Elaine Kirsch Edsall writes a weekly blog www.horsehusband-cancer.com where her eye for often-overlooked detail, and a way of expressing herself that is both thought-provoking and humorous, transform everyday tales of living with life-limiting illness while trying to stay sane into fascinating vignettes of her life.

She lives in the heart of picturesque Dorset countryside, where she buys and sells antiques, and shares a home with her husband, two cats, and her beloved horse Bruce.

Currently, Elaine is working on a book that will combine her lifelong partnership with horses, and her first-hand experience of serious illness.

FB WRITER PAGE:
https://www.facebook.com/ElaineKirschEdsall/

Cynthia Funk

I live in Texas with my husband, two horses and a tenacious Jack Russell. I have an apothecary, Medicine Ranch Botanicals, that is focused on wellness through plant medicine. I also do Equine Sports Massage Therapy called Touch with Intent, combining science and art, focusing on the relationship between biomechanics and deep healing. Combining this with Wholistic practices and 25 years of research and experience this provides a comprehensive wellness program for a beautiful opportunity to heal. The horses and nature inspire my poetry since I tend to have a "poetic" outlook on life! I would love to hear from you at:

mrbcomfort@gmail.com

Kimberly Griffin

I live on my yacht with David, my husband and our two felines Fiona and Bob, near Orcas Island, Washington State, USA. Horses are a big part of my life and I keep two here on the island. Parker, who I have known for 21 years, and Bautisto my friend of only 14 years. Would enjoy telling you more of my stories.

Kswgriffin@gmail.com

Sue Hill

Sue Hill is an English mother of one and grandmother of two. Step mum to three horses and a dog. She lives in the Fens in England – a very rural area where the Postman's visit is the highlight of the day and two tractors constitute the rush hour. She's been stalking Mark Rashid and Crissi McDonald over the last 11 years and her obsession has taken her to Colorado on countless occasions as well as North Carolina, Seattle and Alaska. She's also visited New York (with a normal friend – yes, she does have a couple) and San Francisco as her husband's suitcase valet. Her husband is not a fan of travelling and it's very handy that he stays at home to look after the animals, so she generally travels alone which gives her time to ponder on the peculiarities of her surroundings. By day she is an accountant, but she asks you not to judge her on that fact. Just to prove that she is slightly normal, she has also been a saddle fitter for the last 17 years. If you ever meet her, just give her a hug, feed her cake, make her a proper cup of tea (PG Tips, boiling water and real milk) and she'll be your friend for life. She is best known for her accurate use of the word "salubrious."

Susan Hannah Hull

After more than 40 years as a clinical psychologist, I find that, while I adore retirement, I miss giving my opinion multiple times a day, so I have started writing. Letters to the editor, comments on social media, memoir, poetry, you name it. I have moved to the country where I roam the hills with my dog and spend hours with my horses every day. A native New Yorker, I moved to Texas to marry and never looked back. I believe I have finally created the life I was meant to live. You can contact me at:
hullsusan@sbcglobal.net

Marian Kelly

Marian Kelly grew up in Memphis, Tennessee before heading downriver to New Orleans, where she earned her doctorate in literature. She now lives on a small farm nestled in the foothills of the Great Smoky Mountains, which she shares with assorted equines and felines, along with the occasional llama. She is passionate about supporting local agriculture and local bookstores, and about, as Krista Tippett would say, bringing love into the center of our politics and economy. Things that bring her joy include going barefoot, dancing, and listening to her old New Orleans radio station WWOZ.
marianthecontrarian@gmail.com

Chris Kent

Chris has written three non-fiction books published between 2017- 2019. *Hounds Who Heal; You, Me and ADHD* and co-authored *The Power of the Human Canine Bond* with Marie Yates. In 2019 she compiled and published a collection of stories, poems, and photographs from people who had never been published before that explored the bond between dogs and their humans called *K9 Connections*. When not running the award winning K9 Project Chris can generally be found at home with her six dogs, five horses, reading, walking in the countryside and enjoying nature. You can find more about Chris at www.thek9project.co.uk Her blog can be found at:
https://chriskentatk9.com/2018/04/13/

Susan Ketchen

Susan Ketchen is a writer from Vancouver Island. She lives on a small hobby farm with too many chickens and not enough time. She has previously published a series of young adult novels about a horse-crazy girl with a challenging genetic condition and, more troubling still, well-meaning parents.
www.susanketchen.ca

Amanda Laramore

Amanda-Jane is a Sacred Passage End of Life Doula. She companions souls as they enter the eternal threshold and begin their dying process. Amanda in a part of the conscious death positive movement. She envisions people can be who they are and die in a way that honors them. She is a Mother, Wife and your friend. Amanda and her Husband welcome and support refugees and asylees in their home. Amanda's light shines brightly in the mountains. Music moves her. Peace and grace exist in the presence of her horses. She is a loyal, passionate and courageous Ouma, to Nora and Nash. Amanda is a South African immigrant who has found her home in Colorado. You can contact her at:

amandalovelight1@gmail.com

Abby Letteri

Abby holds a Masters in Creative Writing from the International Institute of Modern Letters, Victoria University of Wellington (New Zealand). Her poetry and essays have been published in literary magazines both in print and on-line. Her memoir, *down they forgot*, traces her American childhood in the turbulent 1960's and 70's, and will be forthcoming in 2021. She divides her time between a small farm with eleven horses, 2 dogs and a geriatric cat and a home in town with her filmmaker/astronomer husband. She shares the farm with her daughter, a classics scholar and fellow crazy horse woman. Life without animals is unthinkable to Abby.

https://horsefarmlife.home.blog

Ann Levy

Ann Levy discovered the magic of books as a child and has loved reading ever since. She is a stay at home mom but travels extensively through books. She began work as a computer programmer but her desire for creativity led her to writing. She is fascinated by the effect everyone has on the world around them. She writes characters with complete personalities made up of both noble intentions and guilty pleasures. Her characters choose how to think and behave for themselves; but her stories live in the resulting consequences. Ann lives in Ohio with her husband, three sons, and dog.

Elizabeth Love Kennon

Elizabeth Love Kennon, equine manager at Hope Reins, is a master life coach, equine facilitated coach, lifelong horsewoman, and author. Horses and the intersection between our broken places and their whole ones, keeps her learning, growing, and sharing. She lives in Raleigh, NC where she enjoys time with her husband, Jeff, and their sons. She can be found at:
www.elizabethlovekennon.com

Kristina Margaret

Kristina lives in Ladysmith on Vancouver Island, is a mother to two boys and works as a Women's Ayurvedic Lifestyle and Sexual Empowerment Coach. When she is not studying or working, she enjoys writing poetry, cooking, gardening, being in nature and creating witchy goods like candles, bath salts and smudge blends. Kristina is outspoken and ambitious, but her heart lies in working with women to empower them to be their best.
www.kristinamargaret.com

Crissi McDonald

Crissi has been giving horsemanship clinics with her husband, Mark Rashid, for the past twelve years. She is a lifelong horsewoman, teacher, writer, photographer, blogger, and since 2017, a certified Masterson Method® practitioner and two-day instructor.

Her dog articles have been published in *The Bark*. Crissi's writing and photographs have appeared in several of Mark's books and multiple horse publications around the world. She is currently a columnist for the UK's Horsemanship Journal.

Her first self-published book, "Continuing the Ride: Rebuilding Confidence from the Ground Up" was released in 2019. Her second book, "Getting Along with Horses: An

Evolution in Understanding" will be released in 2020. She lives in Colorado with her husband, a herd of horses, three dogs, and an elderly cat.

She can be found at crissimcdonald.com

Mary McGinnis

Mary McGinnis, blind since birth, has been writing and living in New Mexico since 1972 where she has connected with emptiness, desert, and mountains. Published in over 80 magazines and anthologies, she has been nominated for a Pushcart Prize, and has three full length collections: Listening for Cactus (1996), October Again (2008), See with Your Whole Body (2016), and a chapbook, Breath of Willow, published by Lummox for winning the poetry contest in 2017. Mary frequently offers poetry readings and writing workshops in Santa Fe and Albuquerque, New Mexico.

Kate McLaughlin

Kate McLaughlin has always loved horses and writing, successfully combining both passions from a young age. An avid book reader and a keen equestrian, Kate became an instructor and had a successful dressage career, but her path changed course once she was introduced to the world of horsemanship. This marked the beginning of a life's work pursuing the art of Vaquero horsemanship whilst documenting her journey riding with Buck Brannaman in the UK. The success of her 'Road to Buck' blog led Kate to write various equestrian publications, expanding her portfolio and reach. Now the editor of Horsemanship Journal and Western Horse UK magazine, Kate is also studying for her MA in Creative Writing whilst writing her first novel.

Kate-mclaughlin.com
Hello@kate-mclaughlin.com

Tessa Pagones

Tessa Pagones spent 25 nonconsecutive years getting a B.S. in Animal Science and then realized she loves animals enough to not work in that field. She has held many roles that include the word "manager," including horse farm manager, Rotisserie Baseball statistics service manager, network and database manager, and currently information technology project manager. She believes that her first job, shoveling manure in exchange for the opportunity to ride horses, prepared her well for all of her career choices. Tessa is a cat person turned dog lover, and she writes about dogs, cats, horses, family, life, and death in her blog, Daily Dog http://dailydog.blog/. She lives in Westminster, Maryland with her spouse, 3 horses, 3 dogs and one cat.

Celeste Reich

Celeste Reich spends her days as a veterinarian and the rest of her time as a horse loving, animal rescuing writer. She lives in Florida with her equine ophthalmologist husband Dennis and their many dogs, cats, horses, and an occasional owl. Her friends call her Bo. You can find her blog at:
https://itsalwaysanewmoment.wordpress.com/.

Alyssa Revels

Alyssa Revels is a wife, mother, language lover, and Air Force officer. Currently serving as an English teacher at the United States Air Force Academy, she lives in Colorado Springs with her husband, son, and two pups.

Paula Romanow

Paula Romanow started to write as a young child and has never really stopped. Writing has been a constant thread through an eclectic career path that has included working as a musician, journalist, documentary film and television news producer / director, military public affairs officer, and most recently as an academic researcher and lecturer, as well as a social justice and animal rights activist. She has published many newspaper and magazine articles, has written two theses, numerous academic articles and reports beyond measure. It's only recently however that she has returned to her first love, fiction. Paula currently works at St Francis Xavier University in Antigonish, Nova Scotia, surrounded by rescue dachshunds.

Louise Thayer

Louise Thayer was raised in Wales with her twin sister Catherine and she now calls Colorado home. She works with rescued horses at a sanctuary in the foothills of the Rockies and writes, mostly poetry, in her spare time.

Poetry especially was her connection to sanity following several decades of mental turmoil in which nothing much made sense but for the sanctity and scarcity of words in lyrical order. She credits her mum, Sue Thayer, for her love of language and for always having faith in her work.

Lauren Woodbridge

Lauren Woodbridge is a horse trainer, martial artist and farmer from the southern tablelands in NSW. She has been an avid reader and writer since she could speak and spends her time when not working by writing short stories for her kids and extended family and poems for all occasions. She also enjoys eating, sleeping and going on adventures with her young family.

She is currently working on a novel based on her real-life childhood adventures riding a ragtag band of horses across Australia.

laurenwoodbridge@hotmail.com

Kirsten Elizabeth Yeager

Kirsten was born and raised in the fabulous northern suburbia of Northglenn Colorado. Fortunate to grow up at a barn with the other wild stable girls, she forged her love of horses at a young age. Introverted and socially distant, she's found that writing, drawing, and dogs are the only outlets to find sanity. Somehow ending up in the automotive world for the last 29 years, she spends her time looking for car parts and rolling her eyes at mechanics.

She also did a twenty-year stint as a tattooist. When she's not stuck in the garage, you'll find her out on some Colorado lake, with the man of her dreams, a little tequila, and a whole lotta sunshine. Someday, she hopes to live on a lake in Minnesota, rescue a couple dogs, and live happily ever after with her Dreamboat.

ACKNOWLEDGMENTS

We wish to thank the women who have trusted us with their writing, knowing it's nothing less than trusting us with their hearts. Many of our authors have only dreamt of seeing their work published. Whether this is their first time being published, or their hundredth, when we lift our words in print it's both thrilling and humbling. We are grateful to the authors for contributing their authentic voices.

Thank you to our editors at Birch Bark Editing. MaxieJane Frazier, you went above and beyond to help us and our writers, and for that we offer our utmost gratitude. Cat Parnell, your guidance and knowledge were so appreciated on this project. Your editorial polish makes this anthology that much shinier thanks to your skills and heart. Start to finish, it's been a privilege to work with both of you.

We also honor and acknowledge all the women who have come before us. We may not know their names or the sound of their voices. What we do know is they spoke their words to illuminate and elevate our understanding. Through the millennia, there have been women who have spoken out against oppression, abuse, ignorance, and shame. We honor those who came before, as we do the voices we share today. May this tradition of respect continue as we yield to the women who will come after us. May we always share in the knowledge of the strength of our combined experience, and our combined beautiful presence in this world.

CPSIA information can be obtained
at www.ICGtesting.com
Printed in the USA
FSHW020027151120
75825FS